MASSES OF FORMAL PHILOSOPHY

Other books by Automatic Press ♦ $\frac{V}{I}P$

Formal Philosophy
edited by Vincent F. Hendricks & John Symons
November 2005

Thought$_2$Talk: A Crash Course in Reflection and Expression
by Vincent F. Hendricks
September 2006

Political Questions: 5 Questions for Political Philosophers
edited by Morten Ebbe Juul Nielsen
December 2006

Philosophy of Technology: 5 Questions
edited by Jan-Kyrre Berg Olsen & Evan Selinger
January 2007

Game Theory: 5 Questions
edited by Vincent F. Hendricks & Pelle Guldborg Hansen
March 2007

Philosophy of Mathematics: 5 Questions
edited by Vincent F. Hendricks & Hannes Leitgeb
June 2007

Normative Ethics: 5 Questions
edited by Jesper Ryberg & Thomas S. Petersen
June 2007

Legal Philosophy: 5 Questions
edited by Ian Farrell and Morten Ebbe Juul Nielsen
August 2007

MASSES OF FORMAL PHILOSOPHY

edited by

Vincent F. Hendricks

John Symons

Automatic Press ♦ $\frac{V}{I}$P

Automatic Press ♦ $\frac{V}{|}$P

Information on this title: www.formalphilosophy.com/Masses

© Vincent F. Hendricks and John Symons 2006

This publication is in copyright. Subject to statuary exception
and to the provisions of relevant collective licensing agreements,
no reproduction of any part may take place without
the written permission of the publisher.

First published 2006

Printed in the United States of America
and the United Kingdom

ISBN-10   87-991013-3-5   paperback

The publisher has no responsibilities for
the persistence or accuracy of URLs for external or
third party Internet Web sites referred to in this publication
and does not guarantee that any content on such
Web sites is, or will remain, accurate or appropriate.

Typeset in $\LaTeX 2_\varepsilon$
Cover photo and graphic design by Vincent F. Hendricks

Contents

Preface	iii
Acknowledgements	v
1 Ken Binmore	1
2 Alexandre Costa-Leite	9
3 Branden Fitelson	13
4 Donald Gillies	17
5 Paul Gochet	19
6 Valentin Goranko	31
7 Alan Hájek	37
8 Jeffrey Helzner	53
9 Dale Jacquette	59
10 Mark Jago	83
11 Edwin Mares	93
12 Greg Restall	97
13 John F. Sowa	105
14 Alasdair Urquhart	117
15 Heinrich Wansing	119
16 Dag Westerståhl	129
17 Jan Wolenski	135

18 John Woods	141
About the Editors	149
About Formal Philosophy	151
Index	154

Preface

Masses of Formal Philosophy is an outgrowth of last year's *Formal Philosophy*. In that book we gathered the responses of some of the most prominent formal philosophers to five relatively open and broad questions in the hope of initiating a discussion of metaphilosophical (or methodological) themes and problems surrounding the use of formal methods in philosophy.

The response to *Formal Philosophy* was immediate and surprising. The most important feature of this response was the level of interest among philosophers in the project of rethinking the role of formal approaches to philosophy. We were wrong to think that we needed to initiate a discussion. The discussion was already well underway. All that was missing was the venue which *Formal Philosophy* in part provided. The best philosophers are deeply engaged with the metaphilosophical questions and are eager to voice their views in a relatively informal setting. The masses were ready and after having annouced the sequel where everybody could take an interview we are proud to present you with the *Masses of Formal Philosophy*.

------------------ ♦ ------------------

Taken as a whole, *Masses of Formal Philosophy* serves as a portrait of the discipline at an interesting and important moment in its history. Since the contributors to this volume are and have been helping to shape the future of philosophy it is useful and interesting to have a sense of their view of the enterprise.

As with *Formal Philosophy*, our purpose in *Masses* is not to articulate any specific agenda or definition of analytic philosophy. Rather, it is intended to provide a venue for the discussion of how formal philosophers understand their enterprise. The interview format has the virtue of allowing respondents the freedom to express their general views on metaphilosophical questions without having to provide the kind of rigorous and lengthy defenses of those views that might be demanded, for instance, in the context of a journal article. The responses should therefore be taken for what they are: the candid views of philosophers on the character of formal approaches to philosophy. The contributions collected will become targets for criticism, but more importantly we hope that they can serve as starting points for more sustained investigation and development.

Vincent F. Hendricks & John Symons
Copenhagen and El Paso
October 2006

Acknowledgements

We are particularly grateful to the contributors for devoting time to writing such erudite, enlightening and often thought-provoking interviews and grateful to the philosophical community in general for showing interest in this project. In addition we would like to express our gratitude to Christopher M. Whalin and Elizabeth Pando for proof-reading the manuscript and to our publisher Automatic Press ♦ $\frac{V}{I}$P, in particular senior publishing editor V.J. Menshy, for continuing to take on these 'rather unusual academic' projects.

Vincent F. Hendricks & John Symons
Copenhagen and El Paso
October 2006

1

Ken Binmore

Professor

University College London, UK

Why were you initially drawn to formal methods?

This is an easy question for me, because I began my professional life as a mathematician, working mainly in classical analysis. I had no thought of getting into economics or philosophy when I joined the LSE Statistics Department in 1969. Two of the nine papers I had then written were on statistical subjects, and the statisticians who hired me perhaps hoped to make a statistician of me. If so, they were disappointed, since I remained true to my training in pure mathematics until some years after I was promoted to LSE's Chair of Mathematics in 1975. Some of the textbooks I wrote during this period are still in use [Binmore 77, 80, 81, 82]. It was only when taking stock of my career in 1980 after finishing a term as Chairman of the LSE Statistics Department, that I realized that I had written no mathematical paper for some years. Instead, I was writing papers about the economics of bargaining.

The story of my conversion to economics is a typical example of a random walk. For a long time, my nearest approach to economics lay in having written a paper about sequences of i.i.d. random variables whose average diverges to infinity [Binmore and Katz 68]. But I gradually began to pick up the tricks of the economics trade as a consequence of sitting in on research seminars in mathematical economics with a view to finding out what kind of mathematics economics undergraduates ought to learn. After a while, I read a book or two (Debreu's *Theory of Value* was the first!). Eventually, the time came when I decided that I could do better than last week's seminar speaker, and so wrote some papers on Arrow's impossibility theorem [Binmore 75, 76]. But I didn't regard these papers very seriously, and it wasn't until I began to get interested in developing the ideas on game theory that I had been teaching for a number of years that my loyalty to mathematics began to crumble.

I don't recall the year in which I first began to teach game theory at LSE. I can remember being told by economic theorists at the time that game theory was a failed research programme in which nobody took any interest any more. It must therefore have been five or more years before the revival of game theory that led to what I hope is a permanent rethinking of the foundations of microeconomics. At the time, I had no inkling of what was to come. Indeed, I was more than a little disgruntled when my mathematical colleagues explained that I had a duty to teach the game theory course after the mathematician who had been teaching it resigned, because it was my idea to include such a course in the curriculum. However, I took Von Neumann and Morgenstern's *Theory of Game and Economic Behavior* [Von Neumann & Morgenstern 44] with me on a sailing trip, and I am perhaps unique in having read it from cover to cover while storm-bound in Cherbourg harbor. I had always enjoyed playing Poker, and so Von Neumann's analysis of his two Poker models was of particular interest. The amount of bluffing he claims to be optimal in his second model is so enormous that I felt Von Neumann must have got his mathematics wrong, but by the time I eventually convinced myself that he was right, I found that I was hopelessly hooked on game theory.

It was not until a long while later that I found that I had been influenced, not just by the economists at LSE, but also by the philosophers. When I arrived, Karl Popper's reputation was sky high, and so I attended philosophy lectures and seminars without any thought of their having any impact on my professional career. Karl Popper [Popper 45] himself was startlingly different from my image of the author of *The Open Society and its Enemies*. The only philosopher I had read at the time who had noticed that Plato's *Republic* is a celebration of totalitarian ideals turned out to be unacceptably authoritarian himself. However, I got on well with Imre Lakatos. He did not show much interest in my thoughts on philosophical matters, but I enjoyed our occasional excursions to neighborhood bars.

Another influence of which I thought little at the time was that of Paul Cohen, who spent a year or so in London after proving the independence of the Continuum Hypothesis. He awoke in me an enduring interest in logic and the foundations of mathematics, although he had no interest whatsoever in evangelizing. When I asked him what aroused his interest in the Continuum Hypothesis, he told me that he only chose to work on the subject, because it seemed the easiest of Hilbert's remaining problems. My own interest in the foundations of game theory dates from this time, although I cannot say that my attempts to employ the Turing halting problem and the like to this end has generated much enthusiasm amongst other game theorists.

What example(s) from your work illustrates the role formal methods can play in philosophy?

I think that those who insist that only formal reasoning can be worthwhile make a bad mistake. An axiom-theorem-proof format is designed to close the mind against irrelevancies, but all too often it closes the mind before everything that is relevant has been included in the model. However, there are areas—especially controversial areas—within which formal reasoning is the only way to settle rival claims. For example, I recently contributed to a controversy sustained by a small school of philosophers who tell stories involving imaginary instruments of torture with a view to demonstrating that rational preferences need not be transitive. The paper refutes one of the claims of this school by giving a formal counter-example in which the hypothesis of the argument are satisfied, but not the conclusions [Binmore & Voorhoeve 03].

More generally, I do not see how it would have been possible to make sense of the theory of knowledge required in game theory without formalizing the necessary axioms (as the modal logic **S5**). This is particularly so in the case of the vital notion of common knowledge. David Lewis understood that it sometimes matters that one can iterate the requirement that everybody knows something as often as one chooses, but the world had to wait for Robert Aumann's formalization of the idea in finite terms before it became possible to know for sure what follows and what does not follow from the requirement that something is common knowledge. I think it particularly important that David Lewis [Lewis 69] was wrong to claim that coordinated action is impossible for rational agents unless that a convention to coordinate in this way is common knowledge [Binmore & Samuelson 01].

By a nice irony, David Lewis's [Lewis 76] formalization of subjunctive conditional reasoning in terms of possible worlds similarly puts paid to Aumann's [Aumann 95] claim that common knowledge of rationality implies that rational players will always follow the backward induction path in a finite game of perfect information [Binmore 96b, 96c].

Equally fraught differences arise from the theory of rational decisions put together by Leonard Savage [Savage 51]. This is one of those subjects on which people find it very hard to separate what reason dictates from what their heart's desire. All kinds of folly can therefore flourish unless formal proofs are offered for the claims that are made. One particularly famous difference arose between Harsanyi [Harsanyi 77] and Rawls [Rawls 72], the former claiming that an analysis of rational bargaining in the original position leads to a utilitarian outcome and the latter that it leads to an egalitarian outcome (as envisaged in Rawls' difference principle). This is a battle that Rawls was bound to lose, because the reasons he gives for iconoclastically rejecting Savage's theory show that he does not really understand the theory properly. This is not to say that Rawls' intuition was not sound [Binmore 05], but it cannot be good philosophy to defend right conclusions with wrong arguments.

Finally, I want to mention the idea of an equilibrium, both in rational game theory and in evolutionary game theory. Equilibrium is a vital concept for understanding how societies hold together, but it is a measure of how slippery the notion is that nobody seemed to understand David Hume [Hume 39] on this subject, and it was not until John Nash [Nash 51] offered a formal version of the idea that it was able, as I believe, to take its proper place as the fundamental principle underlying both moral and political philosophy [Binmore 05].

What is the proper role of philosophy in relation to other disciplines?

I am not very excited by subjects like the "philosophy of biology" or the "philosophy of mathematics". I think that biologists, mathematicians, and other specialists are often right to think that writings in this vein have little useful to offer. Nor am I much taken with the kind of philosophy that asks what Aristotle or Kant really meant to say when they seemed to be saying something entirely different. The kind of philosophy that turns me on is what one might call pre-science—the exploring of topics that are not yet sufficiently well understood to count as science.

I understand that focusing on philosophy as pre-science can be frustrating for academic philosophers, partly because some of its best practitioners are not officially philosophers and partly because such a focus denies philosophers the right to regard themselves as experts. After all, how can one be a philosophical expert if solving a problem converts it from a topic in philosophy to one in science? However, I think the hunt for an elusive quarry makes the activity worthwhile for its own sake, whether or not your success is marked up to your credit or that of your profession.

What do you consider the most neglected topics and/or contributions in late 20th century philosophy?

My experience is not sufficiently wide to say anything very general on this topic, and so I will mention only four topics close to my heart.

The first topic is the invitation proffered by John Mackie [Mackie 77] in his ground-breaking book *Inventing Right and Wrong*. After demonstrating that traditional ethics is a castle built in the air, he asks us to think scientific thoughts based on the facts uncovered by anthropologists and the theorems proved by game theorists. But who is willing to take up this gauntlet, when your only reward for turning your back on the moral absolutism of Plato and Kant is likely to be the disdain of your colleagues?

The second topic is John Harsanyi's [Harsanyi 77] renewal of the attempt to discover sound foundations for utilitarianism, which were left in such disarray by John Stuart Mill. Here is a case where the work of one of the great philosophers has been almost entirely negelected because of his use of (not very sophisticated) formal methods. Robert Hare offers Harsanyi some uncomprehending respect, but he seems otherwise to be ignored—except by John Broome in his previous incarnation as an economist. But whenever Jeremy Bentham and John Stuart Mill are mentioned, there too belongs the name of John Harsanyi.

The third topic arises in decision theory. Leonard Savage [Savage 51], the high priest of Bayesianism, says in one place that it would be "ridiculous" to apply his theory in a large world; in another place he says that it would be "preposterous". But his small-world theory is routinely applied by economists and philosophers alike to large worlds. We need a theory that makes sense in large worlds, which we will not create by piecemeal alterations to Savage's axioms.

The last topic is game theory, on which subject I am sorry to say that philosophers have written a great deal but contributed very little. At one time, they concentrated on the impossible task of proving it to be rational to cooperate in the one-shot Prisoners' Dilemma. Nowadays, it seems that they remain hung up on resolving the so-called Newcomb paradox. Even the otherwise sagacious Brian Skyrms thinks that we need to appeal to the otherwise redundant "causal decision theory" to resolve the difficulties raised by the paradox. However, mathematicians are taught always to ask whether an object exists before examining its properties. In the case of the Newcomb paradox, such an investigation yields the conclusion that there is no game that satisfies its requirements. It follows that there is no Newcomb paradox, and so contradictory conclusions it seemingly implies need not concern us [Binmore 94].

What are the most important open problems in philosophy and what are the prospects for progress?

I do not have anything to add to the preceding answer, other than to agree with the orthodox view that the basic philosophical question is: Why is there something and not nothing? But the prospects of finding a satisfying answer seem no better than in the time of Leibniz.

References

[Aumann 95] R. Aumann. Backward induction and common knowledge of rationality. *Games and Economic Behavior*, 8: 6–19, 1995.

[Binmore 75] K. Binmore. An example in group preference. *Journal of Economic Theory*, 10: 377–385, 1975.

[Binmore 76] K. Binmore. Social choice and parties. *Review of Economic Studies*, 13:459–464, 1976.

[Binmore 77] K. Binmore. *Mathematical Analysis: A Straightforward Approach*. Cambridge University Press, Cambridge, 1977.

[Binmore 80] K. Binmore. *Foundations of Analysis I: Logic, Sets and Numbers*. Cambridge University Press, Cambridge, 1980.

[Binmore 81] K. Binmore. *Foundations of Analysis II: Topological Ideas*. Cambridge University Press, Cambridge, 1981.

[Binmore 82] K. Binmore. *Calculus*. Cambridge University Press, Cambridge, 1982.

[Binmore 94] K. Binmore. *Playing Fair: Game Theory and the Social Contract I*. MIT Press, Cambridge, MA, 1994.

[Binmore 96b] K. Binmore. A note on backward induction. *Games and Economic Behavior*, 17: 135–137, 1996.

[Binmore 96c] K. Binmore. Rationality and backward induction. *Journal of Economic Methodology*, 4: 23–41, 1997.

[Binmore 05] K. Binmore. *Natural Justice*. Oxford University Press, New York, 2005.

[Binmore & Katz 68] K. Binmore and M. Katz. A note on the strong law of large numbers. *Bulletin of the American Mathematical Society*, 74: 49–68, 1968.

[Binmore & Samuelson 01] K. Binmore and L. Samuelson. Coordinated action in the electronic mail game. *Games and Economic Behavior*, 35: 6–30, 2001.

[Binmore & Voorhoeve 03] K. Binmore and A. Voorhoeve. Defending transitivity against Zeno's paradox. *Philosophy and Public Affairs*, 31: 272–279, 2003.

[Harsanyi 77] J. Harsanyi. *Rational Behavior and Bargaining Equilibrium in Games and Social Situations*. Cambridge University Press, Cambridge, 1977.

[Hume 39] D. Hume. *A Treatise of Human Nature* (Second Edition). Clarendon Press, Oxford, 1978. Edited by L. A. Selby-Bigge. Revised by P. Nidditch. First published 1739.

[Lewis 69] D. Lewis. *Conventions: A Philosophical Study*. Harvard University Press, Cambridge, MA, 1969.

[Lewis 76] D. Lewis. *Counterfactuals*. Blackwell, Oxford, 1976.

[Mackie 77] J. Mackie. *Ethics: Inventing Right and Wrong*. Penguin, London, 1977.

[Nash 51] J. Nash. Non-cooperative games. *Annals of Mathematics*, 54: 286–295, 1951.

[Popper 45] K. Popper. *The Open Society and its Enemies*. Routledge, London, 1945.

[Rawls 72] J. Rawls. *A Theory of Justice*. Oxford University Press, Oxford, 1972.

[Savage 51] L. Savage. *The Foundations of Statistics*. Wiley, New York, 1951.

[Von Neumann & Morgenstern 44] J. Von Neumann and O. Morgenstern. *The Theory of Games and Economic Behavior*, Princeton University Press, Princeton, 1944.

2
Alexandre Costa-Leite

Assistant Researcher
Swiss National Science Foundation
University of Neuchâtel, Switzerland

Why were you initially drawn to formal methods?

My first contact with formal methods occurred when I was studying Popper's book *Conjectures and Refutations*. I discovered the induction problem and then I decided that I should study Hume's work to understand it. The *Enquiry Concerning Human Understanding* showed me that, indeed, we have good reasons to accept that the world is contingent. My interest in empirical sciences were, therefore, destroyed because I was looking for answers that could not be false. At this time, I came back to the study of mathematics and logic because I supposed that I would discover the most general structure of reality and some necessary truths in these areas. I realized that I should study Wittgenstein *Tractatus* because he had proposed a kind of philosophy where formal methods were the main tool. I studied the *Tractatus* and then I felt that it was exactly that kind of thing that I was looking for. Afterwards, I started studying contemporary formal philosophers and when I finished my undergraduate studies I wrote a monograph on Kripke's contributions to philosophy. Afterwards, in my Master's thesis, I studied Fitch's paradox and I proposed a solution to it using some non-classical modal logics.

What example(s) from your work illustrates the role formal methods can play in philosophy?

I would mention, first, the role of methods for combining logics in philosophy. As Gabbay pointed out in *Fibring Logics*, we know that there are complicated statements in natural languages involving a lot of different concepts which cannot be formalized using a very simple formalism. Let me illustrate the problem. Suppose, for instance, that we are trying to determine if the statement "Contingent propositions can be known" is true or not. This proposition has two different non-interdefinable modalities: Contingency and knowledge. Thus, a simple epistemic logic cannot be used. We have to, at least, combine a logic for contingency with an epistemic logic in order to formalize the statement. Recently, there are a lot of methods for combining logics. My main research consists in applications of those methods in epistemology and metaphysics. I show how they can help us in the analysis of different philosophical problems, principles and concepts such as skepticism and some paradoxes.

Second, I would mention my project called philosophical categorification. Logic is a powerful tool which philosophers utilise to better understand their problems and concepts. As it is well-known, the relationships between logic and category theory (in the sense of Mac Lane) appear in different levels: 1) logical operators can be represented in categories, since objects are propositions and morphisms are proofs (for instance the works of Lambek and Goldblatt); 2) logics can also be assumed as objects of categories where morphisms are translations (for example, some articles of Carnielli and Coniglio); 3) methods for combining logics are universal constructions in some categories where objects are logics (the approach developed by Sernadas and Caleiro). Indeed, there are in the literature some other examples of how category-theoretic concepts can replace logical concepts. However, given that logic is a very important tool in order to understand concepts from philosophical areas such as epistemology and metaphysics, a natural conjecture is that category theory can also play an important role in philosophy. Category theory is a tool which can be used in philosophical theories and itself has an ontological status (some attempts of applying categories in philosophy are those of Badiou, Marquis, Rodin and Reyes). Philosophical categorification is the philosophical counterpart of categorification introduced by some mathematicians (Dolan and Baez), but replacing logical concepts for categorial concepts, and also set-theoretic notions by category-theoretic notions in order to investigate philosophical concepts.

What is the proper role of philosophy in relation to other disciplines?

Philosophy can play a very important role especially in the process of generating news ideas and concepts. Also, philosophy helps in the analysis of main concepts of a given discipline. I should select an example: Take the role of philosophy in mathematics, especially because this is a book on how mathematical methods can be applied in philosophical issues. Why not the converse process? Consider a mathematician who studies the concept of *set* and argue that sets are generated by a certain axiom. The mathematican decides to mathematically develop then an axiomatic set theory. When a mathematician examines the nature of a given axiom, its ontological content, why a set is really a set, how can we know the properties of a set and many other foundational questions, then philosophy is playing a role.

What do you consider the most neglected topics and/or contributions in late 20th century philosophy?

On one hand, the applications of category theory in philosophy and the study of the philosophical content of categories are the most neglected topics in late 20th century philosophy. However, there are other hard problems which have been neglected and that will be probably forever neglected at least in the academic level: The meaning of life, what is death, etc. The formal philosopher just ignores such problems. Maybe formal philosophy can even help in the treatment of complicated philosophical questions.

On the other hand, one of the most important contributions on how formal methods can play a role in philosophy is Kripke's argument that there are necessary *a posteriori* truths (necessary truths which can only be known *a posteriori*). This was a real revolution in philosophy, given that necessity was always related to *a priori* knowledge. This kind of philosophical progress was just possible because formal tools such as modal logic were playing a special role. Another contribution which should be mentioned is possible worlds semantics. Nowadays it is difficult to find a philosopher who does not use such a tool.

What are the most important open problems in philosophy and what are the prospects for progress?

This is a very interesting question. I think that the most important open problems in philosophy is to present some concrete examples of philosophical categorification and show that, therefore, category theory is a very general, abstract and important philosophical tool. The problem of generating a system of ontology (answering questions such as what is an object? what is a property? what is an adequate criteria of existence etc.) using category theory is one of the most important open problem which can be solved. Some other examples are: How to define metaphysical and epistemic modalities without using possible worlds semantics? How to define the notion of contingency in a categorical approach?

However, there are real open problems, much more important than any other problem of any area of science, that no solution has been announced for centuries and looks like that the situation will not change in the near future: What is the meaning of life? What is death?

3

Branden Fitelson

Assistant Professor of Philosophy
University of California at Berkeley, USA

Why were you initially drawn to formal methods?

My father is a theoretical physicist (and a passionate one at that). I have many memories of fascinating conversations we have had about physics and mathematics over the years. For instance, once, when I was 12, we were on one of our frequent road trips between Syracuse and Brooklyn, and my father found a novel way to keep me occupied. "Consider the Earth-Moon system," he said. "In that system, of course, angular momentum is conserved. Moreover, the rate of the earth's rotation tends to slow over time, owing to non-conservative forces. So, why," he asked, "does the system maintain its total angular momentum by increasing the radius of the moon's orbit around the earth? Why doesn't the rate of the rotation of the moon increase instead?" That was a fun road trip. I'm still not sure I really know how to answer his question. Because I found my father's world of mathematical physics so interesting, I was naturally drawn to formal methods. Indeed, I studied primarily mathematics and physics until my junior and senior years at the University of Wisconsin, when I was lucky enough to stumble into some elective philosophy of science and logic courses with Mike Byrd, Ellery Eells, Malcolm Forster, and Elliott Sober. Once I took those first courses in philosophy of science and logic, I was hooked. And, I've never looked back. Indeed, I found the group of philosophy teachers in Madison so intellectually nutritious, that I went on to do my graduate work there (and what a wise move that turned out to be!). I suspect that my father sometimes wishes that I had taken a PhD in theoretical physics instead. But, because I have maintained my interest in the history and philosophy of physics, we are still able to have enjoyable and useful conversations about his favorite topics (e.g., the interpretation of quantum mechanics and the nature of probability in various branches of physics). I also like to think that he's learned a thing or two from me about formal methods in recent years. But, that's probably just hubris on my part.

What example(s) from your work illustrates the role formal methods can play in philosophy?

There are a great many examples that come to mind here! For instance, I think many results in logic and formal semantics in the 20th century have been of crucial importance for analytic philosophy generally (e.g., Prior's semantics for tensed claims, and Kripke's semantics for modal claims stand out vividly in my mind right now). Aside from the many breakthroughs in formal semantics and logic, the great formal work on the foundations of inductive logic and probability (by the likes of Keynes, Hempel, Carnap, Popper, de Finetti, Jeffrey, Skyrms, and others) is also of non-trivial importance, I'd say. This tradition has been continued in the recent flurry of work in formal epistemology generally. Of course, since much of my own research has been focused in these areas, I am thoroughly biased toward them. However, I think of formal methods as being potentially quite useful in many (if not all) areas of inquiry. To my mind, it is (inter alia) the increased rigor, clarity, and systematicity that can be afforded by the use of formal methods which makes them so important. Of course, with clarity and rigor can also come oversimplification and error. But, as the modern mathematical sciences have taught us, formal methods can have deep and lasting intellectual value, so long as they are used in a judicious way. As I see it, the use of formal models can be just as fruitful in philosophy as it is in science. In this sense, I think philosophers are just scratching the surface of the usefulness of formal methods. When I teach introductory formal logic, I always begin with an explicit analogy between formal logic and mathematical physics. In both areas, we are interested in some "natural" (or informal) phenomena, and in both areas we use formal methods to provide rigorous models and techniques for investigating the phenomena in question. To be sure, this involves idealization and (over)simplification in both disciplines. But, this (in and of itself) is no reason to be skeptical about the value of formal methods in either domain of inquiry. There are no naturally occurring frictionless planes with behavior (precisely) matching the theoretical descriptions of mathematical physics, and there isn't anything in natural language that (precisely) corresponds to the "if ... then ..." of classical truth-functional logic. In neither context should the lack of (perfect) fit between formal models and "natural" systems cause one to think that formal methods do not have a significant (and "deep") role to play. I would urge extending this analogy (with care, of course!) to most (if not all) areas of inquiry.

What is the proper role of philosophy in relation to other disciplines?

I suspect that philosophy is most useful to researchers in other disciplines when it helps them to clarify the conceptual (and pragmatic) structure of their discipline. In this way, I think (or hope!) that philosophy departments (still) have an important role to play at the modern university. The philosophy department should be the voice of clarity and plain common sense. And, the philosopher should be a person that can (in principle) talk to just about anyone on campus and help them to get clearer on what they are doing (and why). If a philosopher is involved in an inter-disciplinary project (something that I think more philosophers should be doing, by the way!), he or she should be the person who's always asking things like "what are we doing, anyway?" and "does this make any sense?" While this can often be annoying to one's collaborators, I think it is (when done properly and seriously) essential to intellectual progress. Perhaps this is just naive, but I do think there will always be a central place in the world of inquiry for the philosopher if they can play this role of the wise and sane colleague who is open to constructively discussing the conceptual (and pragmatic) foundations of all areas of investigation.

What do you consider the most neglected topics and/or contributions in late 20th century philosophy?

I think that there are many topics that have been prematurely abandoned or sidelined, and that there are many topics that need much more attention from philosophers (and other researchers). Off the top of my head, I would say that relativism (especially in semantics, but also elsewhere) is a topic that has been overly neglected (although, in recent years, it is making a comeback, thanks to the efforts of John MacFarlane and others). Also, I think inductive logic (and not necessarily just in a Carnapian sense) is a topic that has been prematurely abandoned by mainstream philosophers of logic, probability, and science (and often not for very good reasons). This is something that I've been working on for some time. A few others are working on inductive logic (e.g., Patrick Maher), but there seems to be a general lack of excitement about it in recent years. Finally, I would say that the general problem of language-variance or language-sensitivity is something that should be better appreciated among philosophers of science and formal philosophers generally. Many things that seem (on the surface) not to depend on choice of language actually do (on closer inspection). Here, in addition to the infamous work of Nelson Goodman, I think the work of David Miller on the language-variance of judgments of predictive accuracy and verisimilitude should be more widely read and appreciated by philosophers. It seems to me that these sorts of considerations have implications for many areas of philosophy (especially, philosophy of science and formal philosophy generally).

What are the most important open problems in philosophy and what are the prospects for progress?

I see the proper integration of non-deterministic and probabilistic ideas into the foundations of both science and philosophy as one of the major problems that really needs more attention. We are still, for the most part, stuck in a theoretical world dominated by deterministic / deductive models (of a rather simple kind), and we are just beginning to grasp some of the more subtle implications of truly non-deterministic / probabilistic phenomena. I think there will eventually be a conceptual revolution of sorts involving this shift. But, we are still some distance away from that today. These kinds of prejudices/inertial modes of thought are very deeply rooted and will take many years (if not generations) to be relaxed. However, I do remain optimistic about this. I think significant progress will be made in the coming years.

4

Donald Gillies

Professor of Philosophy of Science
and Mathematics
Department of Science and Technology Studies
University College London, UK

Why were you initially drawn to formal methods?

I took up philosophy because of my great admiration for Bertrand Russell who was my hero at the time (the early 1960's). Russell advocated formal methods for philosophy, and so I naturally assumed that was the right approach.

What example(s) from your work illustrates the role formal methods can play in philosophy?

The most successful example of the use of formal methods from my own work is the introduction of intersubjective probability. This depends on a mathematical proof of extreme simplicity which yet throws some light on the relation between individual and group belief. Without formal methods this result could not have been obtained. For details see my book: *Philosophical Theories of Probability*, Routledge, 2000, pp. 169–75.

What is the proper role of philosophy in relation to other disciplines?

I will here only answer for philosophy of science and mathematics since I have studied other branches of philosophy, such as ethics, but little. I think that philosophy of science/mathematics can interact fruitfully with science/mathematics. The development of science/mathematics can pose new philosophical problems and throw light on old ones. This can lead to valuable developments in philosophy which in turn can prove helpful for the further development of science and mathematics, and so on. I have given an example of this process in a paper with Yuxin Zheng from Nanjing University: 'Dynamic Interactions with the Philosophy of Mathematics,' *Theoria*, vol. 16/3, pp. 437–59.

What do you consider the most neglected topics and/or contributions in late 20th century philosophy?

Undoubtedly Popper has been the most unfairly neglected philosopher in the late 20th century. Almost the only people to take any notice of him are right-wing politicians of a Thatcherite persuasion. Yet he has a great deal to offer philosophers whatever their political persuasion is. He has interesting views on corroboration, the interpretation of probability, on philosophy of mathematics (the theory of World 3), etc. Yet these are rarely mentioned or discussed. One very interesting claim Popper made was that Marxism is metaphysical rather than scientific. Yet I know of no work written in the last thirty years which even mentions, let alone discusses, this claim. Isn't this something of considerable importance for world history?

What are the most important open problems in philosophy and what are the prospects for progress?

I am sure there are many important open problems in philosophy. So I'll here just mention one group of problems which is what I'm working on at the moment. For most of the twentieth century, philosophy of science focused on physics and topics in medicine were rarely discussed. This raises the question of whether many of the standard views in philosophy of science which were developed for physics are applicable to medicine either directly or perhaps in a modified form. There is quite a lot of interesting material to be considered here and a good hope of progress. It might seem that medicine is rather far away from formal philosophy, but it should not be forgotten that there have been some quite successful attempts to write AI programs to carry out medical diagnosis. So medicine too is entering the formal sphere to some extent.

5
Paul Gochet

Professor Emeritus
University of Liège, Belgium

How I was initially drawn to formal methods

In the *Tractatus Logico-Philosophicus* (London 1922) Wittgenstein writes: 'the fact that propositions of logic are tautologies *shows* the formal-logical properties of language and the world (6.12).' In his *Philosophical Investigations* (Oxford 1953), language ceased to be seen as the *great mirror* of Reality. Wittgenstein focuses on language as a medium of communication between agents and introduced the seminal concept of language-game. In *Word and Object* (Cambridge Mass. 1960) Quine took over Wittgenstein's early concern with the referential work of language but he denied *propositional logic* the role of revealing the scaffolding of the world.

For Quine the task of delivering synthetic truths about the structure of reality as a whole belongs to empirical theories regimented in the *canonical notation of first-order logic*: 'the quest of a simplest, clearest overall pattern of canonical notation is not to be distinguished from a quest of ultimate categories, a limning of the most general traits of reality.' Philosophy is continuous with science and differs from it only by the breadth of its categories.

The privileged position that Quine granted to first-order logic was fully justified in 1960. At that time, modal logic could not compete with first-order logic. It had no semantics (except the algebraic semantics developed by B. Jonsson and A. Tarski which had passed unnoticed). One year before the publication of *Word and Object*, distinguished logicians and philosophers such as Lemmon and Henderson could still raise the question: 'Is There Only One Correct System of Modal Logic?' (*Aristotelian Society*, S.V. 1959).

A major advance in formal semantics deprived first-order logic of its privileged status for philosophical inquiry: the invention of *possible worlds semantics* by Kanger, Hintikka, Kripke, Bayart and Guillaume in the late fifties and early sixties. The invention of possible worlds semantics sparked off an *unprecedented application of formal methods*: Montague's complete formalization of large portions of natural language.

Switching from first-order extensional logic to higher order intensional logic, Montague showed that an extensive fragment of English could be rigorously translated into the formalism of intensional logic with types and that a possible world semantics could be spelled out so as to provide intensional logic with a model-theoretic interpretation which satisfies the requirement of compositionality and explains how, as Witttgenstein puts it, 'a proposition can communicate a new sense to us by using old expressions.' This pionnering work was done in 1970 and edited in a book format by Thomason (*Formal Philosophy*, New Haven 1974).

Let me open a quick parenthesis to show the relevance of Montague's formalism outside philosophy. Using the above-mentioned results and methods in *Logique pour le traitement de la langue naturelle* (Paris 2001), Ph. Delsarte and A. Thayse have succeeded in proving that queries to databases expressed in French can be translated into logical formulas and that the latter can in turn be translated into the formalism of a query language for a database such as *Datalog*. Hence the possibility to query data bases in natural language is an unexpected offspring of Montague's formal philosophy.

In one of his papers, whose title sounds like a *manifesto* ('English as a Formal Language'), Montague makes a startling claim. He writes: '... if φ and ψ are logically equivalent sentences ... then "John believes that φ" and "John believes that ψ" will turn out also to be equivalent.' This claim is counter-intuitive and when I say that, I am not appealing to *subjective intuition*, hence I do not lie open to Gellner's charge against 'philosophy by frisson.' The findings I mention below can be cross-checked and repeated at will.

Let φ be the sentence; 'For all individuals x and y if x has the property P and y has it also then $x = y$' and let ψ be the sentence; 'There is an individual x such that for all individuals y, x has the property P if and only if $y = x$.' These two formulas are logically equivalent but the proof that they are so defies human agents and requires the assistance of a theorem prover in the same way as the solution of the four colours problem did (I owe the example to R. Demolombe). Can we expect that if John believes the first sentence he also believes the second? Clearly not. The computational resources of human agents are bounded.

Montague was, of course, well aware of the counter-intuitive claim he had made and proposed a *distinguo* to reconcile it with common sense. We ought to distinguish, he said, between two analyses of beliefs. If beliefs are construed as taking *propositions* as their objects, we should endorse the counterintuitive inference reported above. Logical equivalence qualifies as a good criterion of propositional identity. But if we analyse beliefs as taking *sentence-meanings* as objects, then propositional identity boils down to synonymy. The latter notion however raises problems of its own which will be examined below.

Meanwhile, logicians kept on searching for a *formal criterion of propositional identity* which would neither ascribe logical omniscience to the agents nor take into account their varying and contingent intellectual skills. In a chapter of *Logic, Thought and Action* (Berlin 2005), edited by D. Vanderveken, a new criterion of propositional identity is spelled out within the framework of an axiomatic system. It is based on the notion of *strong implication*. The latter is construed as a relation of partial order which is paraconsistent, finite and *a priori* known. A problem remains open: Is an axiomatic system, sophisticated as it may be, powerful enough to to capture *all and only* the inferences that human agents endorse?

A. Kaplan evinces his misgivings about that very contention: 'describing belief realistically with a purely axiomatic approach is clearly infeasible—the axiomatization would have to be as complex as the human brain itself.' As an alternative, he stipulates that there is some algorithm that believers use for reasoning, and then, without choosing a particular algorithm, he explores the logical properties of belief that result from imposing various constraints on the algorithms (*Esslli* 06).

Examples of applications of formal methods in epistemology and moral philosophy

Since Plato's *Theaetetus*, knowledge is analyzed as *justified true belief*. The founder of epistemic logic, Hintikka, and his followers concentrated on the true belief component of knowledge but did not treat justification as 'a first-class citizen' to use J. van Benthem's phrase. (Gochet & Gribomont, 'Epistemic Logic' in the *Handbook of History of Logic*, vol. 7, Amsterdam 2006).

In a paper published in 2005, S. Artemov and E. Nogina filled the gap and spelled out an axiomatic system for justified knowledge together with an appropriate semantics. Along with assertions such as $K\varphi$ (φ is known), their logic contains assertions of the form $t.\,\varphi$ (t is a justification for φ) where t is an evidence term which can be an evidence constant a, b, c or an evidence variable x, y, z or complex expressions built from the latter by three basic operations (the binary operations *application* and *union* and the unary operation of *inspection*). The logic of justified knowledge rests on the following plausible assumptions: (1) each axiom has justification, (2) justification is checkable, (3) justification assertion of a statement implies knowledge of this statement, (4) any justification is compatible with any other justification (Artemov & Nogina, 'On epistemic logic with justification' in. R. van der Meyden, editor, *TARK* 2005).

Plato's definition was the target of a famous counter-example. Imagine that a man is looking at a dog in a field and mistakes it for a sheep while there is a sheep in the field which our man does not see. The sentence 'There is a sheep in the field' is true. Moreover it is believed and it is evident for the agent. Yet it is not known.

It is remarkable that in the axiomatic system of epistemic logic with justification set up by Artemov and Nogina, 'the foundational Gettier problem of augmenting the tripartite Justified True Belief definition of knowledge becomes a formal epistemological issue.' Even when the formal methods do not solve philosophical issues, they make your assumptions clear and as Artemov puts it, enable you to agree to disagree.

Moreover the development of epistemic logic with justification led to the discovery of new principles in epistemology. Consider the axiom of negative introspection which reads as follows: 'If sentence φ is unknown, it is known to be unknown.' That axiom encapsulates Socratic wisdom: the agent knows the limits of his knowledge.

For all its apparent reasonableness, the axiom of negative introspection has unexpected and highly counter-intuive consequences. It entails 'if φ is unknown to be unknwon then it is known' and finally, applying axiom **T** (namely '$K\varphi$ implies φ'), we get: 'if φ is unknown to be unknown then φ is true.' However, as Artemov observes, the following hybrid version of the axiom of negative introspection holds in the logic of justification: 'if there is no evidence x for φ then it is *known* (in the sense of *knowable*) that there is no evidence x for φ.' Hence epistemic logic yields a new and unexpected principle in epistemology.

Artemov's and Nogina's paper shows the relevance of epistemic logic for epistemology. Looking at the relationship between epistemic logic and epistemology from the opposite angle, V. F. Hendricks inquired into the relevance of epistemology for epistemic logic. In *Mainstream and Formal Epistemology* (Cambridge 2006) he raised the following two questions: (1) Which epistemic axioms are validated by the definition of knowledge in terms of 'convergence in the limit?' (2) Does the validity of the epistemic axioms depend upon enforcing methodological recommandations or structural features of the learning mechanisms?

The convergence concept of knowledge validates the axiom of epistemic logic known as the 'axiom of positive introspection' (If φ is known, φ is known to be known). Hendricks says in *The Convergence of Scientific Knowledge* (Dordrecht 2001): 'if the method correctly converges to φ, the method correctly converges to the conjecture that it converges to φ.' If however we take into account the findings of computational epistemology we have to qualify our assent to the latter principle. Somebody whose hypothesis has begun to converge may lack any reason to believe that it does. To cater for this possibility and to vindicate positive introspection we should, as Hendricks suggests, adopt the *diachronic reading* of the conditional 'If φ is known, φ is known to be known' and allow its consequent ('φ is known to be known') to obtain only *later than* the antecedent.

As far as the negative introspection axiom is concerned, the convergence account of knowledge turns it into a patent falsity, whether it is read synchronically or diachronically. As Hendricks observes, if knowledge is defined by convergence then it contrapositively follows that if you have not converged you do not know and, in particular, it follows that you *do not know* that you have converged.

Deontic logic is another field in which very fruitful applications of formal methods to philosophical issues can be found. A short paper published in *Analysis* by R. Chisholm the same year as Gettier's paper on the definition of knowledge stirred the whole community of logicians and analytically-minded moral philosophers by confronting them to the following paradox: 'Let us suppose: (1) it ought to be that a certain man go to the assistance of his neighbours; (2) it ought to be that if he does go he tells them he is coming; but (3) if he does not go then he ought not to tell them he is coming; and (4) he does not go.' This apparently innocuous set of statements generates a plain contradiction if we apply the straightforward principle of distributon of 'ought' over 'if ... then ...': 'if it ought to be that a occur and if it ought to be if a occur then b occur, then it ought to be that b occur.'

Just as mathematicians did not discard Russell's antinomy as a *do not care*, but looked for remedies (type theory or axiomatic set theory), we should be wary of this paradox especially as it brings to the fore a major philosophical insight: It is a fact of everyday life that agents do not always conform to the norms. Hence secondary norms are needed which indicate, as J. Carmo and A. Jones say, 'what is to be done in circumstances in which actual behaviours have deviated from the ideal' ('Deontic Logic and Contrary-to-Duties,' forthcoming).

The discovery of Chisholm's paradox had a highly positive effect. It set up new standards of adequacy for deontic logic. It became clear that a system of deontic logic has to show which actual obligations are derivable in circumstances of violation of some primary obligations without, for that matter, making it impossible to derive the ideal obligations.

To meet these standards a new semantics is needed in which it is possible to represent the distinction between *actual obligations* and *ideal obligations*, and moreover to represent violation itself. For that purpose two notions of necessity (and correspondingly two notions of possibility) are needed: What is *actually* fixed, given what the agents have decided, and what *could not have been avoided* no matter what the agents had done. This requires, the authors of the paper show, that we bring in two kinds of worlds: The set of worlds which are the *open alternatives* of the current world and the set of worlds which are the *potential versions* of the current world. The next stage consists, of course, in the setting up of an axiom system which is sound and complete with respect to the semantics which has just been sketched.

These important technical aspects should not detain us here. The question I want to address is, 'what can moral philosophers learn from this kind of investigation?' Twenty years ago, in *Mérites et Limites des Méthodes logiques en Philosophie* (ed. J. Vuillemin, 1986). B. Williams claimed that deontic logic had shed 'no light on any interesting question of moral philosophy' and he complained that 'it had turned attention away form the considerations of social philosophy and the philosophy of mind that are needed for an understanding of these matters.'

With the benefit of hindsight, we can now see that B. Williams' criticisms against deontic logic have lost much of their bite. As J. Carmo and A. Jones observe, systems of laws are human artefacts which are likely from time to time to give rise to conflicts of obligations. Formal systems are set up to prevent that eventuality and to restore consistency whenever inconsistency occurs. As to the relevance of philosophy of mind for deontic logic, it should neither be underrated nor overrated. The relation of preference, which belongs to philosophy of mind, psychology and economics, is expected to play a role in any model built up to represent contrary-to-duty imperatives. It turned out, however, that the model spelled out by J. Carmo and A. Jones had no need for that relation.

I do however agree with B. Williams that there are insuperable conflicts of obligations which no methods, be they formal or not, can remove. As N. Harmann writes: 'The alternative is not between wrong and right, but between wrong and wrong. Either way a value is violated ... Whoever stands in such a predicament ... cannot escape without offence' (*Ethik*, Berlin 1926).

The proper role of philosophy in relation to other disciplines

The first encounter between Analytic philosophers and Continental philosophers took place in Royaumont (France) in 1958. To Jean Wahl, who asked him whether philosophy is an island or a promontory, Austin replied that it rather looks like the surface of the sun, 'a pretty fair mess,' which deals with all residues, all problems which remain unsolved after we have tried all established methods to tackle them. As soon as a safe method has been discovered, Austin continues, a new science takes shape and looses itself from philosophy. Austin envisions that some time in the future an amalgamation bringing together grammar, linguistics, logic and psychology might give rise to a new science which would encompass problems belonging to philosophy today (*La Philosophie Analytique*, Paris 1962, C.E. Caton, *Philosophy and Ordinary Language*, Illinois 1965).

Clearly Austin wants to avoid being impaled on the horns of Wahl's dilemma. He balks at the idea that philosophy could be an *island*. Indeed the island-metaphor implies that philosophy is an isolated discipline which has its own methods. This idea has been condoned by some. There are philosophers who advocate *a special access* to Reality – Post-Kantians spoke of 'intellectual intuition,'

Bergson of 'metaphysical intuition,' Whitehead of 'metaphysical induction' – but those philosophers never reached agreement with their peers as opposed to the philosophers who relied on commonsense and scientific method only. Austin also rejects the idea that philosophy could be a *promontory*. He refuses to grant philosophers a *privileged position* from which they can criticize scientists, artists or politicians. On both scores I fully agree with Austin.

I am not convinced however when he suggests that philosophy is a *pre-scientific* branch of learning which continually dissolves into science. There is room for a philosophical investigation of sciences which scientists themselves do recognize as legitimate. Consider, for instance, the philosophy of mathematics.

In *Set Theory and Its Logic* (Harvard 1963) Quine succeeded in providing a foundation for the principle of mathematical induction which does not require that we postulate an actual infinite set of individuals contrary to what many mathematicians and philosophers thought. Admittedly we still need larger and larger classes without end but as Quine stresses, 'they can all be finite.'

The axiom of infinity will prove indispensible at a later stage, namely for the theory of real numbers but it is important to know exactly which portions of mathematics requires which objects. This is a philosophical question if any. Remember Ockham's precept: 'Do not multiply abstractions beyond necessity.' In *Set-Theory and Its logic*, Quine answers it *from within science*. His purpose is, as L. Decock puts it, to show that ontological questions can be genuine scientific questions without ceasing to be philosophical (*Trading Ontology for Ideology*, Dordrecht 2002).

The dissolution of philosophy into science considered by Austin does not occur here. Nor does it in Joëlle Proust's monograph *Comment l'esprit vient aux bêtes?* in which a philosophical inquiry is conducted on the growth of mental functions with constant use of results from biology, experimental psychology, neurophysiology and cognitive ethology.

Neglected topics in the late 20th century philosophy

The frontal attack launched by Quine against the analytic-synthetic dichotomy in his epoch making essay 'Two Dogmas of Empiricism' (1951) had a positive result. It established a version of semantic holism which, with due qualifications, is generally accepted today. Its significance has sometimes been misunderstood.

Quine's claim that the double dependence of science upon language and experience is not significantly traceable into the statements of science taken one by one led some readers to think that no pure analytic statements remain, except those that are obtained by uniform substitution in logically valid statements (such as 'Every bachelor is a bachelor') but there are also analytic statements of another kind such as 'Every bachelor is unmarried.' These statements have generally been despised as truisms of no interest. Yet some of them are far from truistic.

As Ph. Mongin shows in 'L'analytique et le synthétique en économie' (Louvain, forthcoming), there are statements in economics (and this is also true of other sciences) for which the question arises whether they should be construed as analytic statements (of the second kind) or as synthetic statements. The question is not trivial. The answer we give it has far-reaching consequences in recondite parts of the whole theory of micro-economics. An example of a statement whose status is uncertain is the law of supply and demand which Mongin states in this way: 'for all consumers and for all goods *which are not a Giffen good*, the amount of good demanded by the consumer decreases when the price increases, the other variables remaining fixed.'

I side with Ph. Mongin in making a plea for analytic statements. Even if they are true *ex vi terminorum*, the latter statements can teach us something new although not something new about the world. We can apply to them what Frege said about the statements that we derive from definitions by applying logical deduction: 'these deductions are indeed contained in the definitions but in the way a plant is contained in a seed, not in the way a beam is contained in a wall.'

The notion of synonymy is another notion which has fallen in abeyance and which Ph. Mongin strives to revive. The relation of synonymy is often criticized for being symmetric and reflexive but not transitive. Lacking the property of transitivity, synonymy cannot be an equivalence relation. It immediately follows that the proposal to define proposition as the equivalence class of sentences synonymous to a given sentence made by Russell in *Inquiry into Meaning and Truth* (London 1940) is doomed to failure (See my *Outline of Nominalist Theory of Propositions*, Dordrecht 1980).

The solution to this quandary is twofold. As Mongin suggests we should first take wider units of sense than words or sentences (as Quine himself suggested in 1951), next we should introduce two new parameters: The *context* and the *intentions* of the speaker. *Meaning is context-bound*, whether we take the context to be an article, a book or a whole science. It is also constrained by the intentions of the speaker. This second constraint operates sometimes indirectly when the speaker speaks on behalf of somebody else. Perelman alludes to a situation of that kind when he writes: 'I personally believe that in his interpretation of the law (when the law is obscure or silent), the judge should try to discover the legislator's will ...' (*The New Rhetorics and the Humanities*, Dordrecht 1979).

I said that *meaning* is context-bound. Some Continental philosophers have gone further and claimed that *truth* is context-bound. B. Latour is among them. He rejected the report of French scientists who had examined the mummy of Ramses II and said that he had died of tuberculosis, arguing that the report *was anachronistic* (because the tuberculosis bacillus only came into existence when Robert Koch discovered it in 1882). P. Engel shows that Post-Modernist positions of that kind are self-defeating ('Analytic Philosophy and Cognitive Norms', *The Monist*, 1999).

In *Theories and Things* (Harvard 1981), Quine writes that truth is always immanent to a theory. This does not however entail relativism in so far as Quine requires that we always speak from the standpoint of *the best* theory available to us (see my *Ascent to Truth*, Munich 1986).

An important open problem in philosophy

Where should we draw the border between *logical* and *non logical constants*? This is an open problem which has recently received much attention. Permutation invariance has been used to provide a demarcation of logicality. In 'Logical constants: the variable fortunes of an elusive notion' (*Festschrift for S. Feferman*. ASL Publications 2001) J. van Benthem investigates the virtues and weaknesses of this criterion.

The demarcation between logical and non-logical constants turns out to be elusive. The borderline between logical and non-logical is fuzzy. But unexpectedly, logical constants cluster around a center and the *core invariants* differ from the peripheral ones by the *rich amount of inferences* they warrant.

This result is intriguing. Items which are close to one another *from one angle* can at the same time be distant from one another *from another angle*. It is clear that my geometrical metaphor does not suffice. We need more. I suspect that formal methods will be helpful here in so far as they can go beyond both intuitions and concepts.

Let me conclude with a quotation from J. Ladrière: 'Formal language does not merely sharpen meanings which are already understood .... It itself promotes meaning by its own resources and gives an original access to areas of significance which cannot be explored by other means' ('Le formalisme et le sens', *Les Langages, le sens et l'histoire*, Lille 1975).

6

Valentin Goranko

Associate Professor
School of Mathematics
University of the Witwatersrand, Johannesburg, South Africa

I should begin this interview with a disclaimer. I am only an 'aspiring' philosopher, if any, not a 'real' one by training nor by profession. Yet, I have been a logician ever since my graduate studies, and a mathematician—ever since I remember myself. These, I suppose, could qualify me at least as a potential philosopher. Besides, as we (humans) progress in life, one way or another, we all tend to become increasingly more philosophical, partly in resignation to the complicated and imperfect surrounding world, and partly driven by the instinct to remain sane in it.

After this disclaimer, I can now afford philosophizing at will, hoping that no one will consider too seriously and take me to task for what I say. And, after all, as a wise man put it, some things in life are so serious, that we can only joke about them. If any, Philosophy should be one of them.

Now, to the questions.

Why were you initially drawn to formal methods?

Being a mathematician (at least in my soul) from a very early age, I have *always* been drawn to 'formal' methods, theories, and systems; but in my pre-logical days, these were not 'formalities' for me, they were the Real Thing. Only after being educated in logic I gradually began to think of it, and of the whole of mathematics, as formal methodologies, besides being scientific disciplines of their own right. I still hold these views.

One more circumstance, specific to my youth days in communist Bulgaria: Philosophy, just like any other social science, was so repellently ideologically loaded there, that going formal was a relief and intellectual refuge for any dissenting and non-conformist mind, for whom a formal theory was much more appealing and satisfying than ideological junk.

What example(s) from your work illustrates the role formal methods can play in philosophy?

Personally, I find formal methods, and in particular, formal logic, an extremely comfortable vessel that allows me to wade in deep philosophical waters without drowning in them. A parallel with mathematics and its foundations is natural here: Contemporary mathematics is based on set theory, which itself is based on one or another axiomatic system, usually an extension of Zermelo-Fraenkel set theory, ZF, with the Axiom of Choice. Thus, the question of 'what is true in mathematics?' is conveniently reduced to 'what is true in set theory?', which in turn is replaced by 'what is provable in ZF(C)?'. In particular, many questions on the existence, nature, and types of infinity can be referred to, and resolved within, the theories of ordinal and cardinal numbers, well-developed within ZFC.

Similarly, intrinsically deep and debatable philosophical problems, arguably not amenable to purely philosophical solutions, can be 'settled' by applying formal reasoning on them. Three well-known examples, of different flavours:

1. Zeno's paradoxes are 'killed' by the theory of convergent and divergent series. The role of formal methods (in this case, calculus) here is to replace the unreliable, or even paradoxical, intuition by precise computation and deduction.

2. The eternal discussion on the nature of time can be settled (not resolved!) by adopting one or another mathematical model of the time flow, which reflects one's views, or conventions, of what one means by 'time', and then formally establishing mathematical properties of that model. The role of formal methods here is to provide formal models of debatable or evasive philosophical concepts, and then—axiomatic basis for reasoning and exploration of philosophical issues.

3. While self-referring (circular) definitions of concepts are anathema, or at least non grata, in informal logical reasoning, they can be perfectly legitimate constructs in mathematics and formal logic, as inductive definitions or fixed point constructions, both based on precise and well-developed mathematical theories. Formal methods here enable us to provide

methodology and put on sound foundations intuitively elaborated modes of discourse and reasoning.

Thus, while formal methods do not really solve philosophical problems, they help, first to formulate ('specify') them in a precise, unambiguous, and clear for the non-philosopher way, then—to search for 'formal' solutions, and to test if a proposed solution meets the 'specification'.

Moreover, formal methods and studies can raise, or at least make us aware of, questions and problems that are of philosophical nature, but have not been explicit in the philosophical agendas before. Let me give one example, drawn from my own experience and work, of how formal methods can influence philosophical discourse and analysis. A currently active area of research on the border of computer science and artificial intelligence, in which I have been involved lately, is *logics for multi-agent systems*. This area aims, in particular, to clarify and formalize by means of logical systems, the interaction between actions, knowledge and strategic abilities of agents and groups (coalitions) of agents. In this research endeavor some essentially philosophical issues have surfaced, that seem not to have been much in the focus of attention of philosophy until recently, viz.: *how does an agent's knowledge affects its abilities to perform given actions, and to have strategies to achieve certain goals*. In particular, *can an agent have different abilities to act, or different strategic abilities to achieve a goal, in two possible states of the world which are epistemically indistinguishable for that agent?* Furthermore, *can a group of agents have a collective strategy of achieving a goal, without having a common knowledge of that strategy, or even of the goal?* These questions are closely related to theories of rationality and knowledge. For instance, *what is rational behavior of an agent or a group of agents in conditions of incomplete information?*

What is the proper role of philosophy in relation to other disciplines?

In my view, Philosophy is, and has always been, the nervous system of the body of sciences, connecting them in one organism and enabling vital communication between them. Especially nowadays, when sciences are so much specialized and engulfed in the study of their own aspects of knowledge, Philosophy plays the unique role of a device zooming our minds out of the microscopic facets of the World seen through the other individual sciences and letting us see the Big Picture.

Another crucial role of Philosophy is to ask, and keep trying to answer, the fundamental questions underlying every science, but considered to be too general and transcending its methods and scope, to be resolved within that science. I don't think philosophy's role is to give any definitive answers to questions or solutions to problems; but it should raise and clarify them, and keep prompting the scientists to try to resolve them. To paraphrase a popular adage, Philosophy is not a destination for the Mind, but the journey itself.

A tempting parallel with Gödel's incompleteness theorems comes to the logician's mind here: no sufficiently rich in content discipline can resolve its own fundamental problems within itself, i.e., with its own methods and tools. So, Philosophy comes as the universal Calculus Ratiocinator here. (Well, every logician can now see a self-refereintial paradox looming here: What discipline, then, resolves Philosophy's fundamental problems? The only safe answer in sight: These must be unresolvable, in principle ...)

What do you consider the most neglected topics and/or contributions in late 20th century philosophy?

I do not feel competent enough to answer this question for the entire philosophy, but in my view one of the most neglected questions in Logic, surprisingly, is '*What is the Logic of human reasoning?*'. After all, Logic was allegedly initiated as a study of the modes and laws of human reasoning; but while it has achieved a lot, it certainly has not offered much insight into how we, humans, *actually* reason. All I know for sure on this subject, is that in our thinking we certainly do not follow any explicitly formalized logical system; and in our *really* creative reasoning we necessarily transcend any pre-designed and axiomatically stipulated system of reasoning, for otherwise Gödel's incompleteness theorem would confine us to remain logically correct but intellectually infertile bores. In fact, I think the ability to strictly follow formal logical reasoning can be successfully used as a Turing anti-test: only a computer, but no human being, can efficiently perform resource-complex logical inferences, while never making a single logically unjustified leap of reasoning, that enables us, humans, to reach the previously Unknown. But, what is then Logic about, after all?

What are the most important open problems in philosophy and what are the prospects for progress?

The first that come to mind here is: Surely, one of the most important problems in philosophy is *to identify the most important problems in philosophy*! And, this problem is bound to always remain open, though always with good prospects for progress. Actually, this status should apply to all important problems in philosophy, I think.

On a slightly more serious note, as a mathematician I find that some of the most important and attractive problems in philosophy concern philosophy of mathematics, viz.:

- *What is mathematical truth?* I don't see much positive recent progress on this question since Kant, Frege, and the leading foundationists of mathematics, Russell, Hilbert and Brouwer. Indeed, Tarski invented the formal semantics, but that only shifted the problem from the object language to the meta-language. In fact, he also showed that this question is doomed in a way, since no sufficiently rich mathematical theory can formally capture its own criteria for truth. Furthermore, the spate of independence results in set theory, following Gödel-Cohen's independence of the Continuum Hypothesis from the 'classical set theory' ZFC, the alternative between the Axiom of Choice and the Axiom of Determinacy (inconsistent with each other, yet each claiming to provide adequate foundations for the 'working mathematician'), and the intensive, yet still futile, current search of alternative, intuitively acceptable as true principles in set theory that would resolve these, and other set theoretic conundrums (such as the (non)existence of various large cardinals), strongly suggest that the nature of truth in mathematics may never reach definitive status.

- *What is mathematical reality?* This problem, closely related to the previous one, but even more fundamental, is presently as pertinent and hotly debatable as in Plato's times, and both Platonist and anti-Platonist views and arguments abound in mathematics nowadays.

Let me wind up this answer, and the interview, on a (seemingly) lighter note. One fundamental and tantalizing philosophical question, that we keep asking ourselves throughout our life, is;

What is the purpose of life?

6. Valentin Goranko

We find no commonly accepted and satisfying answer to this question, yet we refuse to put up with the gloomy thought that there isn't any (answer, or worse, purpose of life). So, we keep searching forever, not realizing that by doing so, we are achieving the very answer, since:

The purpose of life is to search for purpose of life!

7
Alan Hájek

Professor of Philosophy

Philosophy Program

Research School of the Social Sciences

Australian National University, Australia

Why were you initially drawn to formal methods?

I came to philosophy as a refugee from mathematics and statistics. I was impressed by their power at codifying and precisifying antecedently understood but rather nebulous concepts, and at clarifying and exploring their interrelations. I enjoyed learning many of the great theorems of probability theory—equations rich in 'P's of this and of that. But I wondered *what is this 'P'*? What do statements of probability *mean*? When I asked one of my professors, he looked at me like I needed medication.

That medication was provided by philosophy, and I found it first during my Masters at the University of Western Ontario, working with Bill Harper, and then during my Ph.D. at Princeton, working with Bas van Fraassen, David Lewis, and Richard Jeffrey—all deft practitioners of formal methods. I found that philosophers had been asking my question about 'P' since about 1650, but they were still struggling to find definitive answers. I was also introduced to a host of other philosophical problems, and it became clear to me within nanoseconds of arriving at U.W.O. that I wanted to spend my life pursuing some of them. But I kept being drawn back to the formal methods of mathematics, and in particular of probability theory.

It may be worthwhile to pause for a moment and to ask: "What *are* formal methods?" Of course, it's easy to come up with examples: the use of various logical systems, computational algorithms, causal graphs, information theory, probability theory and mathematics more generally. What do they have in common? They are

7. Alan Hájek

all abstract representational systems. Sometimes the systems are studied in their own right for their intrinsic interest, but often they are regarded as structurally similar to some target subject matter of interest to us, and they are studied to gain insights about that. They often, but not invariably, have an axiomatic basis; they sometimes have associated soundness and completeness results. There is something of a spectrum of 'formality' here. At the high end, we have, for example, the higher reaches of set theory. At the low end we have rather informal presentations of arguments in English in 'premise, premise ... conclusion' form. Higher up we find more formal representations of these arguments, whittled down to schematic letters, connectives, and operator symbols. Near the top we find Euclid's *Elements;* lower down, Spinoza's *Ethics.*

Formal systems typically facilitate the proving of results about some domain. They often provide a safeguard against error: by meticulously following a set of rules prescribed by a given system, we minimize the risk of making illicit inferences. I was struck by how one could start with a rather imprecise philosophical problem stated in English, precisify it, translate it into a formal system, use the inference rules of the system to prove some results about it, then translate back out to a conclusion stated in English. I liked the rigor, the sharpening of questions and their resolution, and the feeling that one was really getting *results.*

I was also impressed by how formal systems could stimulate creativity. Staring at the theorems of a particular system can make one aware of hitherto undiscovered possibilities, or of hitherto unrecognized constraints (I give an example in the next section.). It can also enable one to discern common structures across different subject matters. For example, Ginzburg and Colyvan (2004) fruitfully emphasize the similarity of the equations of population growth to those of planetary motion (these systems are governed by similar second-order differential equations).

However, one must be careful not to read too much off a given formalism. It may resemble some target in certain important respects, but it must differ from the target in other important respects (Compare how a map of a city differs from the city itself in all sorts of ways—it had better do so in order to be of any use!). And one should resist turning formalism into a fetish—as it might be, representing some philosophical problem with triple integrals and tensors, just because one can.

I can't engage in any such autobiographical reflections without acknowledging the huge intellectual influence of David Lewis on my own research. I found his use of formal methods to be exemplary. I was especially drawn to his work on counterfactuals, on causation, and of course on probability and decision theory. He used such methods sparingly and judiciously, always to illuminate and to make insights easier to come by and to understand. His work serves as a model to me.

What example(s) from your work illustrates the role formal methods can play in philosophy?

My early philosophical work was on probabilities of conditionals. Conditionals are notoriously recalcitrant beasts, having defied adequate analysis for over two thousand years. I liked Adams's and (independently) Stalnaker's idea of looking to probability theory, and in particular its familiar notion of *conditional* probability, for inspiration. They both advanced versions of the thesis that *probabilities of conditionals are conditional probabilities*. Then along came Lewis's triviality results, which began an industry of showing that various precisifications of the thesis entailed triviality of the probability functions. I liked this industry *a lot*, and I joined in, proving some further triviality results.

I became fascinated with conditional probability in the process. I came to have misgivings about the traditional formula for conditional probability as a ratio of unconditional probabilities:

$$P(A|B) = \frac{P(A \cap B)}{P(B)} \quad \text{(provided } P(B) > 0\text{)}.$$

It was well known that this *ratio analysis* runs aground when $P(B) = 0$ (that parenthetical proviso is there for good reason!), yet probability theory admits probability-zero propositions as possible and non-trivial. Worse, the ratio analysis as it stands fails when $P(A \cap B)$ or $P(B)$ are *vague* or *undefined*—yet such cases abound, as I argue at length in my (2003b). To be sure, Kolmogorov refined the ratio analysis to handle the $P(B) = 0$ problem, although his refinement still falters on the other problems. And it faces some further problems of its own, as Seidenfeld, Schervish and Kadane (2001) have shown.

I have also utilized formal methods in my work on Pascal's Wager. I have a tendency to be drawn to big things—the Himalayas, the Empire State Building, the Grand Canyon, Elvis's Jungle Room—and according to Pascal, the utility of salvation is as big as can be: *infinite*. His Wager is arguably the most famous argument for theism. This is a perfect example of how formal methods can be brought to bear on a philosophical problem. Think of the problem of whether or not to believe in God as a *decision problem*, and thus one to be solved by decision theory. Put in modern parlance, Pascal assumes that non-belief and God's non-existence both lead to finite utilities, and that you should assign positive probability to God's existence; he concludes that you maximize expected utility by believing in God. Given his assumptions, Pascal was right: the infinite utility of salvation swamps all other terms in the expectation calculation. But as I have argued in my (2003a), it does not follow that you should believe in God. For given Pascal's assumptions, you *also* maximize expected utility in infinitely many other ways. Any mixed strategy between belief and non-belief scores just as well, by Pascalian lights: the infinite utility of salvation *still* swamps all other terms in the expectation calculation, so these mixed strategies all get infinite expectation too. Moreover, arguably *anything* you could do should be regarded as such a mixed strategy, for there is presumably *some* probability that you will wind up believing in God as a result. Now translating back from the formalism to the real world decision problem: far from establishing that you should believe in God, Pascal's premises apparently have the consequence that *everything* you could do is equally rational. You might as well have a beer—or not. I went on to suggest various ways in which the utility of salvation could be understood so as to render Pascal's argument valid.

The St. Petersburg paradox involves another decision problem that apparently has infinite expectation. A fair coin is tossed repeatedly until it lands heads for the first time, and you get exponentially increasing rewards according to how long it takes (starting at, say, $2 if it lands heads immediately). The paradoxical conclusion is usually taken to be that decision theory judges the game to be infinitely good, whereas intuition recoils at this judgment. But I think a more disturbing conclusion is that, once again, as long as you give *any* credence to the possibility of playing the St. Petersburg game, all of your possible actions get infinite expectation. If decision theory is your guide to action, then like Buridan's ass you are paralyzed.

Expected utilities are *sums*; the St. Petersburg game exploits a certain kind of anomalous infinite sum, one which diverges. But we know from real analysis that another kind of anomalous infinite sum is one that is *conditionally convergent*—if we leave it alone, it converges, but if we replace all of its terms by their absolute value, the resulting series diverges. Riemann's rearrangement theorem tells us that every conditionally convergent series can be reordered so as to sum to any real number; and it can be reordered so as to diverge to infinity and to negative infinity; and it can be reordered so as to simply diverge.

Now let this piece of mathematics guide the creation of a new game, whose expectation series has exactly this property—the formal model thus inspires a new kind of anomaly for rational decision-making. Harris Nover and I (2004, 2006) proposed a St. Petersburg-like game—the *Pasadena game*—in which the pay-offs alternate between rewards and punishment, in such a way that the resulting expectation is conditionally convergent. Decision theory apparently tells us that the desirability of the game is *undefined*, thus falling silent as to its desirability. Worse, the theory falls silent about the desirability of *everything*, as long as you give any credence whatsoever to your playing the Pasadena game—for any mixture of *undefined* and any other quantity is itself undefined. In that case, for example, you can't rationally choose between pizza and Chinese for dinner, since both have undefined expectation (each being 'poisoned' by a positive probability, however tiny, of a subsequent Pasadena game). Thus, once more you are paralyzed—a sin against practical rationality. Yet assigning probability 0, as opposed to extremely tiny positive probability, to the Pasadena game seems excessively dogmatic—a sin against theoretical rationality.

Another body of work in which I appealed to formal methods concerned the so-called *desire-as-belief* thesis. David Lewis canvassed a certain anti-Humean proposal for how desire-like states are reducible to belief-like states: roughly, the desirability of X is the probability that X is good. He then proved certain triviality results that seemed to refute the proposal. This was another lovely example of how formal methods could serve philosophical ends: this time, a thesis that was born in an informal debate in moral psychology could apparently be expressed decision-theoretically. The decision-theoretic machinery could then be deployed to deliver a formal verdict, which could then be translated back to bear on the informal debate.

I noticed that the probabilities-of-conditionals-are-conditional-probabilities thesis of Adams and Stalnaker looked suspiciously like the desire-as-belief thesis, and that Lewis's triviality results against the former looked suspiciously like his triviality results against the latter. This gave me the idea that the subsequent moves and countermoves that were made in the probabilities-of-conditionals debate could be mimicked in the desire-as-belief debate. I showed that, much as Lewis's original triviality results could be blocked by making the conditional *indexical* in a certain sense, his later triviality results could be blocked by making a 'good' indexical in the same sense. Philip Pettit and I (2003) then translated back out of the formalism, suggesting meta-ethical theories that accorded 'goodness' the necessary indexicality. So the trick was to notice a similarity between the formal structures that underpinned the probabilities-of-conditionals and the desire-as-belief debates, something that I could not have noticed about the original debates themselves. After that, it was easy to see how the next stages of the desire-as-belief debate should play out, paralleling the way they did in the probabilities-of-conditionals debate. Two seemingly disparate debates turned out to be closely related.

So I have come full circle back to my original work on probabilities of conditionals. I am in the process of writing a book on the two debates, and their many structural similarities, in a book to be entitled *Arrows and Haloes: Probabilities, Conditionals, Desires, and Beliefs*.

What is the proper role of philosophy in relation to other disciplines?

An ongoing side-project of mine is to gather philosophical heuristics, analogues of 'castle early and often' in chess. A useful one is to see the word 'the' in neon lights. A locution of the form '... the X ...' typically carries with it the presupposition that there is exactly one X, and this presupposition may well be false. Suitably cautioned by the heuristic, I will observe that there are *many* proper roles of philosophy in relation to other disciplines. I would rather not try to order them in importance, or to demarcate their domains.

It's something of a platitude that philosophy is concerned with foundations, although some platitudes are actually true, especially here in my adopted town of Canberra. So whereas a physicist asks about the chance that a given atom decays in some period of time, or a chemist asks about the chemical properties of some compound, or an astronomer asks what causes black holes to form, a philosopher asks "What is chance?", "What is a property?",

"What is causation?" If we do our job well, our answers to these philosophical questions will accord with such canonical applications of these concepts in the sciences. That said, the boundaries between philosophy and other disciplines are somewhat permeable. Where, for instance, is the borderline between philosophical and mathematical logic?

Much of philosophy that I find interesting can be characterized by the slogan: "Making our implicit commitments explicit." These include the commitments of common-sense, familiar to the folk, which almost inevitably infiltrate the sciences to some extent, and even more so the social sciences. They also include the commitments of scientific and social-scientific theories themselves. And philosophy plays a useful role as watchdog of other disciplines: questioning their presuppositions, policing their over-hasty inferences, clarifying their murky concepts. It teases out unintended and often unwelcome consequences of those presuppositions, provides tools for evaluating those inferences, and offers frameworks for understanding better those concepts. This is especially evident in the various 'philosophy of _ _ 's. It is somewhat contingent which disciplines get to fill in the blank. Philosophy of physics has long been a respectable field. Philosophy of biology is rather more recent, but it is currently thriving. Philosophy of chemistry is still at a nascent stage, but it is showing promise. Philosophy of geology, of meteorology, of astronomy, and of other 'special sciences' are yet to arrive on the scene. Perhaps they are not fundamental enough (as are physics and arguably chemistry), and perhaps they do not raise problems of a distinctive enough kind (as does biology) to merit sustained philosophical attention.

Another significant role for philosophy vis-à-vis other disciplines is to address *prescriptive* questions, where they typically address *descriptive* questions. This distinction is often blurred by the near-homophony of the words 'idealization' and 'ideal'. Indeed, sometimes the words get conflated, as when chemists speak of the 'ideal gas law', suggesting a law about maximally virtuous gases, when really it is an *idealized* gas-law. Physics, for example, is up to its neck in idealization, and so is decision theory. But whereas decision theory attempts to codify *norms* and *evaluates* actions that meet them or not, physics just codifies and unifies regularities without approval or sanction. Decision theory exhorts the *ideal* of maximizing expected utility theory, and criticizes us when we fall short of that ideal. But physics never tells an electron that it is irrational, nor a galaxy that it is badly behaved.

7. Alan Hájek

Many good philosophers are like intellectual decathletes, knowing a fair bit of mathematics, science, and social science, with better-than-average writing skills. And every serious discipline has its share of philosophical problems. There is thus much opportunity for cross-fertilization: the other disciplines can offer material for philosophers to sink their teeth into, and the philosophers can offer in return rigorous scrutiny of the disciplines' foundational issues.

What do you consider the most neglected topics and/or contributions in late 20th century philosophy?

Some topics are properly neglected, and some are paid undue attention. But an improperly neglected field is surely the *philosophy of statistics*. As an undergraduate I was schooled exclusively in the tradition of classical statistics, à la Fisher and Neyman-Pearson. It wasn't until I became a philosopher that I even heard of Bayesian statistics, and it's still an area that has been neglected by philosophers. To be sure, philosophical issues in statistical inference and estimation have been addressed in important work by philosophers such as Hacking and Kyburg, and statisticians such as Dawid and Lindley—but again, these have not reached the philosophical mainstream.

My statistics professors taught me about type 1 and type 2 errors in hypothesis testing, and that the former were somehow worse than the latter. But nobody ever recommended the obvious way to avoid the former: set the significance level of a hypothesis test to 0! So I gathered that the former were clearly not infinitely worse than the latter. That left me wondering exactly what the terms of trade were between the two kinds of error. Here statistics meets *decision theory*, yet a course on it was unavailable in my four-year statistics degree. I was also taught that rational inference and decision-making look rather different in a context of strategic interaction among multiple players. Here, presumably, statistics meets *game theory*, although I never heard a word about their union. And I was taught that "correlation is not causation." A catchy slogan, to be sure, and a sound warning—but nothing more was said about causation. Here statistics meets *causal modeling*. I thus see the interfaces between statistics and these more philosophical preoccupations as primary areas of neglect—certainly in my own education, and I surmise in the academy more generally. Cutting edge work in these areas, in turn, should inform debates in some other areas of philosophy. For example, philosophers of mind working on mental causation could profit from keeping up to date with the causal modeling literature.

Many of the debates in philosophy of mind and in ethics are couched in purely deductivist terms. They concern questions such as these: Are mental facts identical to, or reducible to, or supervenient on non-mental facts? Are moral facts identical to, or reducible to, or supervenient on non-moral facts? While Hume denied the intelligibility of necessary connections between distinct existences, philosophers in these areas sometimes talk as if *only* necessary connections between seemingly distinct existences could be of philosophical interest: identity, reducibility, supervenience. Similarly, while epistemology has embraced probabilistic methods, the debates in the philosophy of mind and moral psychology are still mainly conducted using the all-or-nothing categories of 'belief' and 'desire.' Looking on as an outsider to these debates (and confessing the outsider's ignorance), I fear that their protagonists are setting themselves up for failure: they risk stalemating. To be sure, I will cheer as loudly as anyone if their deductivist, all-or-nothingist aspirations are realized. But in the meantime, I think that the debates could use a healthy injection of *probability*.

The concept of probability was a relative latecomer on the intellectual scene—it is entirely absent from the works of the ancient Greeks and medievals. One wonders how such clever chaps could get by without it! But even in the twentieth century we see major philosophical work on probability-laden notions being done without any aid from probability theory—think of Hempel on confirmation theory, or Popper on scientific methodology. We can safely say with the benefit of hindsight that trying to force the round peg of inductivism into the square hole of deductivism is like trying to square the circle. I wonder whether future philosophers will look back on these current debates in ethics and philosophy of mind, conducted as they are entirely in deductivist terms, in a similar way.

Perhaps, then, we would do well to break the philosophy of mind and ethics free of the straitjacket of entailment relations, and seek *probabilistic relations* between physical facts and mental facts, or between physical facts and moral facts. Or said without any pessimism: perhaps we should seek such probabilistic relations first, before shooting for full-blooded entailments. Still more ecumenically, we could productively run both research programs side-by-side. Again, think of how traditional epistemology, trafficking as it does in all-or-nothing concepts such as knowledge and belief, happily co-exists with probabilistic epistemology.[1] Indeed, probabilism offers a way of side-stepping some of traditional epistemology's concerns with skepticism, and of resolving some hoary paradoxes, the lottery and the preface paradoxes among them.[2]

So this is a call to arms to philosophers of mind and ethicists: to arm themselves with probabilistic methods when tackling their traditional problems. Just securing comparative probabilistic supervenience relations would be a good start: "physical basis U makes it more probable that there is a mind than physical basis V does;" "physical basis X makes it more likely that there are moral facts than physical basis Y does," and so on. We could then try to work our way up from there.

Related, philosophers often regard *soundness* of arguments as the only criterion of success, when we ought to know better. Soundness, after all, is neither necessary nor sufficient for an argument being compelling or of value (Now *there's* something that can be said in purely deductivist terms!). Think, for example, of the time-honored philosophical strategy of *parodying* an argument that one doesn't like, as Gaunillo did to St. Anselm's ontological argument, or as Diderot did to Pascal's Wager. We start with the target argument, show that it is 'just like' another argument with an obviously silly conclusion, and which is thus obviously unsound, and conclude that the target argument must likewise be unsound. Setting aside the manifest unsoundness of *this* line of reasoning—tu quoque!—it mistakenly regards soundness as the touchstone of argument assessment. And it surely proves too much. The sensible argument

All emeralds so far observed have been green
The next emerald will be green

is 'just like' the silly argument

---

[1] Let me put in a plug here for the annual *Formal Epistemology Workshop*, created by Branden Fitelson and Sahotra Sarkar, which has done much to bring together epistemologists from both traditions. See:
http://socrates.berkeley.edu/~fitelson/few/

[2] That said, we need to understand better the interrelations between the probabilistic and the non-probabilistic concepts. It seems that the 'knowledge', 'belief', and 'evidence' defy purely Bayesian analysis. Rather, the Bayesian eschews the first two notions, and takes the third for granted.

All emeralds so far observed have been grue
The next emerald will be grue

where we define 'grue' so as to make the conclusion obviously false. And indeed, both arguments are unsound, just as the proves-too-mucher would have it. But again, what is needed is a healthy injection of probability—in this case, a confirmation theory that can account for the obvious difference in inductive strength between the two arguments.

To be sure, the proves-too-much strategy is often a useful heuristic, and it is even more often dialectically and rhetorically effective. I am not above using it myself—I did so, for instance, in my paper "Scotching Dutch Books?" But while we're at it, notice that the strategy seems to regard the parody argument, as it were, as a *template* for a kind of bad argument, and the strategy regards any argument that fits the template well enough as automatically bad. Here I am reminded of Massey's important insight in a number of papers (e.g. Massey 1975) that, trivial cases aside, there is no such thing as invalid argument *form*, the way that there is such a thing as valid argument form—no schema or template for arguments, any instance of which is invalid. These papers by Massey are high on my list of underappreciated contributions to philosophy.

Looking elsewhere, *information theory* is apparently flourishing — witness its popularity in cognitive science, computer science, and engineering. Yet the *philosophy of information theory* is so unflourishing as to be virtually non-existent. And I suspect that information theory, and specifically minimum message length theory, may offer just the right tools to address some old philosophical chestnuts—for example, quantifying the extent to which true scientific theories balance simplicity and strength, and thus the extent to which they can be regarded as codifying the *laws of nature* on the Mill-Ramsey-Lewis analysis (Dowe and Hájek 1997). This is surely fertile, and under-harvested, philosophical ground.

Computer simulations bring with them another set of philosophical problems that have not received sufficient attention. What is the epistemological significance of 'experiments' that are performed on one's laptop? How do simulations relate to thought experiments? To what extent should applied ethics pay attention to simulations—for example, to computer models of global warming or of overpopulation? And closer to my home turf, to what extent are Monte Carlo methods faithful to the probabilistic models that inspire them?

Finally, there are hard questions in meta-philosophy that do not receive sufficient attention. Conceptual analysis is thought by many to have passed its use-by date, although it is regarded as alive and well in my adopted town. When should a concept be taken to be primitive, and when is it an appropriate target of analysis? More generally: What should philosophers be doing, and how should we be doing it? Such topics are occasionally addressed, but usually in a somewhat piecemeal fashion—an article here or there on this or that topic in meta-philosophy. Bravo to Vincent F. Hendricks and John Symons for stimulating profitable and sustained dialogue addressing such methodological questions in their volumes.

What are the most important open problems in philosophy and what are the prospects for progress?

This very nearly reduces to the question: "What are the most important problems in philosophy ...?"—for very few important problems in philosophy are *closed*. Gödel's proof of the incompleteness of arithmetic is taken to be a canonical example, although it is arguably more a piece of mathematical logic than of philosophy. I take philosophy to have definitively settled various *negative* results: almost any significant piece of conceptual analysis has eventually met with decisive counterexamples. It's *positive* philosophy that's really difficult.

I won't pretend to give an exhaustive list of *the* most important open problems (that word again!). But I'll mention some obvious ones and then say rather more about some of the problems that grip *me* the most.

First, some obvious ones: the mind-body problem; the nature of consciousness, and of free will; the rationalist / empiricist debate over innate ideas; the existence of God; Plato's problem of the one and the many; the existence of abstract objects; the status of moral facts; the status of modal facts; the meaning of 'meaning'; the content of 'content'; a true analysis of 'truth'; the problems of induction ("old" and "new"); a proper understanding of a 'just' society; the nature of time, and its relationship to space; and (dare I say it), how we are to live good lives. Take a look at the curriculum of your typical undergraduate philosophy program, and you'll see a menu of such topics.

Much as the holy grail for physicists is a grand unified theory of physics, the holy grail for me is a *grand unified theory of rationality*. This would be nothing less than a fully integrated decision

7. Alan Hájek

theory and confirmation theory that incorporates the insights of statistics, game theory, and causal modeling, and that explicates rational judgment, preference, and action at both the individual and group level.

Let's start with individual rationality. I imprinted on Bayesianism in my philosophical infancy, but like a rebellious child, there is much that I now question in it. Its central notion is that of *degree of belief*, or *credence*, but I find the main analyses of this notion to be inadequate (the betting interpretation and other forms of operationalism, interpretivist accounts that appeal to a decision theoretic representation theorem, and so on). I find equally inadequate the main lines of defence of Bayesianism: the Dutch Book argument, the representation theorem argument, calibration, and so on. So, much as I admire the theory for its elegance and for its fruits—its explanatory power, its ability to illuminate various old problems in confirmation theory, and its unification of confirmation and decision theory—I believe that its foundations could use some shoring up.

Then there are questions about the very statement of Bayesianism. It tells us that credences should conform to probability theory — but what does that mean exactly? Should credences be defined on a sigma field, or does a field suffice? Should they be countably additive, or does finite additivity suffice? How exactly should the 'normalization' axiom be formulated? If formulated sententially, it takes the form 'all tautologies receive probability 1'—but tautologies of which logic? If classical logic, do we mean propositional logic, predicate logic, predicate logic with identity, or more? Are non-classical logics permitted? If not, why not, and if so, which ones? Should conditional probability be defined in the usual way as a ratio of unconditional probabilities, or as I prefer, as a primitive? How do we extend our theory of conditional probability to uncountable probability spaces? And so it goes.

All of this presupposes that we know what the arguments of probability functions are in the first place, but here again there is work to be done. For example, a currently burgeoning subfield of research, prompted by problems of self-location such as the 'Sleeping Beauty' problem, concerns whether the contents of probability assignments should be *centered* propositions, and if so, what the 'centers' should be. Again, there are foundational issues aplenty.

Now take the notion of 'credences' as given, and let's agree that they should conform to the probability calculus (whatever that means exactly), just as the Bayesian says. Demanding though this norm is—*you* try assigning probability 1 to all tautologies!—in other respects it is far too permissive. In particular, we need further reasonable constraints on priors. I have misgivings about the details of some of the main proposals, although I am sympathetic to their spirit. They include:

- *Regularity*, an unevocatively named 'open-mindedness' constraint to assign probability 1 only to tautologies. Since regularity is the converse of the normalization axiom, stating the former exactly is problematic in the same ways as the latter is.

- The *Principal Principle*, the more evocatively named constraint that says, roughly, one's credence for a proposition should equal one's subjective expectation of its objective chance. Yet we lack an adequate account of objective chance in its own right.

- The *Reflection Principle*, the equally evocatively named constraint that, roughly, one's credence for a proposition should equal one's subjective expectation of one's *future* credences of it. Yet there are apparently various cases in which this principle fails—e.g., those involving memory loss, or even merely epistemically possible memory loss, and indexical beliefs.

- The *principle of indifference*, and more generally, the *principle of maximum entropy*, that roughly say that one should assign the 'flattest,' least informative probabilities that one can, consistent with one's evidence. A major worry is the apparent partition-dependence of applications of these principles.

Here the subjectivist interpretation of probability begins shading off into the logical interpretation. I regard getting right the details of these principles, and of additional such principles, as a high priority. After all, whether we like it or not, our epistemic practices betray our commitment to a quasi-logical notion of probability. We think that it would be irrational to deny that the sun will rise tomorrow, to project 'grue' rather than 'green' in our inductions, and to commit the gambler's *fallacy*. Understanding this irrationality takes us to the very heart of confirmation theory.

Subjective probability plays a key role both in confirmation theory and in decision theory. And we find yet more turmoil in the foundations of decision theory. Firstly, we need to sort out the inter-mural disputes between various rival decision theories—in particular between so-called 'evidential' decision theory and the variants of causal decision theory (which themselves seem far from equivalent to me). Then there are paradoxes to be resolved. High among them for me are the paradoxes associated with the St. Petersburg game and the Pasadena game.

We need to understand better the relationship between decision theory and game theory. Decision theorists tell us that rational action is always, everywhere, and without exception a matter of maximizing (their preferred version of) expected utility. Yet game theorists talk instead of Nash equilibria, sub-game perfect equilibria, proper equilibria, trembling hand equilibria, and so on in contexts of strategic interaction with others agents (not to mention their distinction between games in normal and extensive form). To what extent are these just different ways of saying what the decision theorists say, and to what extent do our theories of rationality bifurcate depending on whether we are playing games against nature, or against other agents? (And where do we draw the line for what counts as other agents? When I am interacting with my dog Tilly, am I playing a game against nature, or against another agent? It often seems like a bit of both.)

Matters are complicated further when we take into account the *moral* aspects of our decision-making—as we often must—when we are uncertain about which meta-ethical theory is correct. Kantianism says that Jim must not shoot one Indian to stop Pedro from shooting twenty, while utilitarianism says Jim must. Suppose Jim is 50% confident of the truth of each theory. What should he do? And how do we incorporate the deliverances of such theories into decision theory? For example, if a Kantian categorical imperative can be mapped onto a utility scale at all, it would appear to correspond to a negative infinite utility—and we are saddled again with St. Petersburg-style paradoxes, and corresponding paralysis. Andy Egan and I (MS) are exploring such issues further.

These problems are only writ larger when it comes to aggregating the opinions and preferences of multiple agents, let alone an entire society. Important relationships between rational individual and cooperative group choice are being explored by authors such as Isaac Levi, Christian List, Robert Nau, Philip Pettit, Brian Skyrms, and the Carnegie Mellon trio of Joseph Kadane, Mark Schervish, and Teddy Seidenfeld. But again, there is much further work to be done.

And if all that could eventually give us a modicum of guidance on how we are to live good lives, all the better—although I'm not holding my breath.[3]

Dowe, David and Alan Hájek (1997): "A Computational Extension to the Turing Test", *Proceedings of the 4th Conference of the Australasian Cognitive Science Society*, Newcastle, NSW, Australia.

Egan, Andy and Alan Hájek (MS): "Moral Uncertainty".

Ginzburg, Lev R. and Mark Colyvan (2004): *Ecological Orbits: How Planets Move and Populations Grow*, New York: Oxford University Press.

Hájek, Alan (2003a): "Waging War on Pascal's Wager", *Philosophical Review*, Vol. 113 (January), 27–56. Reprinted in *The Philosopher's Annual* 2004, ed. Patrick Grim, www.philosophersannual.org.

Hájek, Alan (2003b): "What Conditional Probability Could Not Be," *Synthese*, vol. 137 (December) 273–323.

Hájek, Alan and Philip Pettit (2004): "Desire Beyond Belief", *Australasian Journal of Philosophy*, Vol. 82 (March), 77–92 (special issue dedicated to the work of David Lewis). Reprinted in *Lewisian Themes: the Philosophy of David K. Lewis*, eds. Frank Jackson and Graham Priest, Oxford University Press, 2004, 78–93.

Hájek, Alan and Harris Nover (2006): "Perplexing Expectations", *Mind* 115 (July), 703–720.

Massey, Gerald (1975): "Are There Any Good Arguments that Bad Arguments are Bad?", *Philosophy in Context* 4, 61–77.

Nover, Harris and Alan Hájek (2004): "Vexing Expectations", *Mind*, Vol. 113 (April) 237–249.

Seidenfeld, Teddy, Mark J. Schervish, and Joseph B. Kadane (2001): "Improper Regular Conditional Distributions", *The Annals of Probability*, Vol. 29, No. 4 (October), 1612–1624.

---

[3] I thank especially Carrie Jenkins, Aidan Lyon, and Daniel Nolan for helpful discussion.

8

Jeffrey Helzner

Assistant Professor of Philosophy
Columbia University, NY, USA

Why were you initially drawn to formal methods?

After dropping out of college several times I moved to Boston in order to study music composition with the composer Randall Woolf. Conversations with my musician friends as well as some honest introspection allowed me to recognize that I was more interested in and inclined towards the structural aspects of music than music itself. This recognition led to my mathematical studies. Shortly after this transition I had the good fortune of meeting Ethan Bolker. Though supportive of my mathematical interests, Bolker recognized that I might be better suited in areas that are more clearly foundational or philosophical than what is common in mathematics proper. Thus, Bolker kindly arranged for me to meet with Richard Jeffrey at Princeton. My meeting with Jeffrey opened my eyes to other possibilities. Before that meeting I had no idea that there was such a thing as mathematically processed philosophy. Looking back, I can imagine this sounds odd, but one can major in pure mathematics (e.g. algebra, topology, and analysis) without hearing much mention about Russell, Frege or how investigations into the foundations of mathematics have played a role in the development of analytic philosophy.

Despite the interesting world of ideas described by Richard Jeffrey, I decided at that time to continue with mathematics rather than study philosophy. With this decision I went to Buffalo in order to study category theory with F.W. Lawvere. Listening to Lawvere lecture on logic and category theory had a profound influence on me. Since my meeting with Jeffrey I had been reading books on mathematical logic. However, I never felt comfortable with what I found to be a very linguistic and often combinatorial approach to logic; I have always been more of a right-brained, visual-spatial person. Lawvere emphasized the geometric character of logic and that seemed more natural to me.

From Buffalo I moved to Pittsburgh and entered the logic program at Carnegie Mellon, which provided an incredible atmosphere to study mathematically and scientifically informed areas of philosophy (e.g. logic, decision theory). At Carnegie Mellon I continued my focus on mathematical logic in general and category theory in particular. The philosophy department at Carnegie Mellon had several terrific mathematical logicians. Steve Awodey offered excellent courses on topos theory and various topics in categorical logic. Jeremy Avigad kindly provided me with my first real research experience by funding and supervising one of my first summers in Pittsburgh.

Having had some time to think about philosophical matters I came to the conclusion, naive though it may be, that contemporary mathematical logic was concerned more with ontology while my own interests were shifting towards epistemology. During that same period I was starting to learn some decision theory from Teddy Seidenfeld and some philosophical logic from Horacio Arló-Costa. I soon learned about connections between work on rationality and a range of interesting areas (e.g. economics, methodology, AI and cognitive science). The work had a real interdisciplinary flavor, something that I enjoy and that has a well-established tradition at Carnegie Mellon (thanks in large part to visionaries like the late Herb Simon). I was very fortunate to write my thesis under the supervision of Seidenfeld and Arló-Costa. Our regular meetings were, in my estimation, the most important component of my graduate school experience. Trying to integrate Seidenfeld's perspective, more from the foundations of statistics, and Arló-Costa's perspective, more from philosophical logic, was extremely helpful in allowing me to assemble my own views on rationality. In fact, this situation even provided an opportunity for integrating different formal methods (e.g. convex sets and measurement theory from Seidenfeld, relational semantics and neighborhood semantics from Arló-Costa).

What example(s) from your work illustrates the role formal methods can play in philosophy?

Before I respond to your question, let me try to be clear on how I interpret the reference to *formal methods*. As I understand it, work in "formal philosophy" (or, as I sometimes prefer, "mathematically processed philosophy") involves a nontrivial use of structures of the sort that would be recognized by a significant number of mathematicians *and* intended interpretations of these structures such that these interpretations would be recognized as philosophically relevant by a significant number of philosophers. Finding a proper balance between these two factors is not easy. It is an art that derives its quality from the formal philosopher's ability to harness the power of two factors that can pull in opposite directions.

The distinguishing features that I have suggested allow for work in a variety of forms. There are the classic limiting results in logic and the well-known impossibility results in rational choice. There are the translations or mappings between seemingly different areas (e.g. Hans Rott's mappings between belief revision and rational choice). Thought experiments can put pressure on the relationship between a formal model and its intended interpretation—consider any one of several now-famous examples in decision theory. In such cases, the presence of a precise model helps to clarify the range of possible modifications. Finally, a contribution in formal philosophy may involve the distillation of the model itself. Examples of this sort are numerous, but an outstanding example would be something such as Ramsey's analysis of "partial belief" in his "Truth and Probability" from 1926.

As far as something closer to home, let me mention an example that I hope will have, for variety's sake, a flavor that is a bit different from the sorts of things that will be cited in other sections of this volume. Recently, Horacio Arló-Costa and I have been pursuing a research program that questions the explanatory power of the psychological effects paradigm that is employed in many areas of behavioral decision theory; we suspect that the paradigm is limited in important ways by its resistance to indeterminacy. In light of this we revisited some of the psychological responses to examples such as those suggested by Daniel Ellsberg. In work that has now been reported in several talks, we attempted to demonstrate the limitations associated with one of the most well-known psychological responses to Ellsberg's example, namely Fox and Tversky's "comparative ignorance" hypothesis.

In place of Fox and Tversky's explanation, Arló-Costa and I suggested that Ellsberg's own analysis, in terms of tradeoffs between security and expectation, seemed capable of accommodating the data that we used in our case against the comparative ignorance hypothesis. As articulated in Ellsberg's own theory, these tradeoffs are represented as a real-valued parameter. The question is then how does one measure these tradeoffs from some combination of observable behavior and background assumptions? This sort of question has a long and philosophically interesting history, a contemporary account of which can be found in the encyclopedic *Foundations of Measurement* volumes of Krantz, Luce, Suppes and Tversky. In our case, the issue was how to enrich the relevant space of items in such a way as to support a sufficiently unique measurement of tradeoffs. There are well-known sets of axioms that provide for such uniqueness by assuming binary operations (e.g. the concatenation of rigid rods in the measurement of length) or trades betweens attributes in conjoint measurement. Of course, in such an application one must take seriously the interpretation of this enriching structure. The empirical setup that we employed in our pilot study suggested the possibility of applying Herstein and Milnor's very general and elegant "mixture space" approach; essentially, our experimental setup had us taking mixtures over random devices. We are in the process of preparing a pilot study to test our tradeoff model.

What is the proper role of philosophy in relation to other disciplines?

I tend to view the normative character of philosophy as its most distinctive feature. Many of the philosophical projects that interest me the most concern the analysis of concepts that are applied in other disciplines. Of course, I try not to delude myself into believing that the "oughts" derived from such an analysis are always of interest to individuals working in these other disciplines, but the hope is that there is some contribution to a wider effort.

What do you consider the most neglected topics and/or contributions in late 20th century philosophy?

I think that too much of analytic philosophy begins with the asking of "What is ...?" questions. However, as we all know, there are other possible openings: "What does ...?" and "How does ...?" are notable examples. I am not suggesting that alternatives to the "What is ...?" have suffered from complete neglect, but rather that these alternatives suffer from a relative neglect that ought to be rethought given the advances that have been made in certain other disciplines. For example, has philosophy really taken full advantage of the insights that have been offered by the category theorists? Of course category theory has been discussed in connection with the philosophy of mathematics, but I am talking about something wider. It seems to me that category theory suggests and supports a different mode of analysis, one that places emphasis on transformations rather than objects or, as one of my teachers once remarked, on verbs rather than nouns.

What are the most important open problems in philosophy and what are the prospects for progress?

I am not really comfortable with talk of "open problems" in philosophy, at least not without some qualifying remarks. For me, "open problem" suggests a case where it is clear what it would mean for something to qualify as a solution. I do not think that there are open problems in philosophy in the same sense as there are open problems in mathematics. That said, one's philosophical program may reach a state where the precise formulation of certain problems is possible, but in these cases it seems to me that the problem enjoys importance by being a piece of data that is obtained in pursuit of the underlying philosophical program. Now, given these qualifying remarks, do I feel more comfortable answering the question? No, not really.

9

Dale Jacquette

Professor of Philosophy

Department of Philosophy, The Pennsylvania State University, PA, USA

Netherlands Institute for Advanced Study in the Humanities and Social Sciences (NIAS), Royal Netherlands Academy for the Arts and Sciences (KNAW)

Why were you initially drawn to formal methods?

I am more visually than verbally oriented. I get easily confused reading Shakespeare, for example, but not when I attend a performance (others apparently have the opposite experience or are equally confused by both). I suppose that if I couldn't work professionally in philosophy I would consider becoming a photographer. There too I like the neatness and precision of the tasks. My favorite amateur experiences in photography involve capturing sunlight on a work of street art or architectural detail, freezing the moment and preserving something of another person's artistic skill and intentions. I like the technical problems encountered in photography, and I like the idea of solving them mechanically by tweaking the digital information taken on site afterwards in a computer environment to produce a well-composed vibrant color image that makes a pictorial statement.

Like many another logician, therefore, I can report that I was drawn to study logic in part by the 'beauty', or, as I prefer to say, the absorbing visual interest, of logical syntax. This by itself would not have been enough to enlist my energy over so many years. Put together with an appreciation for logic's expressive scope and flexibility, its grammatical and inferential schematizations, and the power of its implications, a better but still incomplete explanation is in sight. I had the vague sense when I first studied the subject as an undergraduate that logic was somehow the most fundamental philosophy-related subdiscipline, and that this impression was somehow related to my grasp of its importance. I still think this is true, although I have yet to work out exactly how or in what sense logic is philosophically foundational. The efforts I have seen to explicate the relation, beginning especially in the era with Gottlob Frege and Bertrand Russell, do not begin to satisfy me, although I feel that they sometimes have a clear glimpse of the situation and were often on the right track.

The problem is not just the metatheoretical failure of classical logicism, or the fact that the 'logic' logicists developed contained hidden mathematical and especially set-theoretical concepts all along. Rather, I find something deeply misconceived about the way in which logicism had hoped to link the intellectual and epistemic importance of modern logic to the larger project of theoretical philosophy. This in turn is related to what later emerged as my primary fascination with symbolic logic. I think that logic informs philosophy as rational discourse in many ways. I remain convinced that the relation does not translate plausibly into projects that pretend to begin with pure logic and only afterward ascend to the plane of theoretical philosophy. I believe the relation to be more integral, amounting to an interdependence between logic and philosophy that does not permit them to be cleanly separated and arranged one above or before the other. I suppose that this is in large part what prevents logic from simply being handed over to mathematics, but keeps it for the foreseeable future squarely within the philosophy curriculum. I agree that we can use logic to build up certain parts of mathematics, as long as at least some mathematical concepts are superadded. By itself, I do not think that this fact establishes any unique or distinctive relation between logic and mathematics. The same can be said in general terms with respect to the use of applied logic in any specialized branch of philosophy, science, or even certain parts of religion or art or literary criticism. Logic by itself, I believe, offers nothing beyond the answers to problems concerning concepts that are already built into a formalism. These can include concepts of objects, properties, predication, identity, truth, and, of course, more obviously, logical relations such as the propositional connectives, quantifiers, and modalities. There are invaluable presuppositions to be quarried from the development of symbolic logic, including answers to basic problems of formal ontology, even when logic is narrowly construed as a 'purely' syntactical formalism. To the extent that we are committed to such a logic, we can unpack a surprising number of interesting implications of these commitments. This, too, has impressed me about the critical study of philosophical logic. What most interested me in my early study of modern logic, however, was none of these things, important as they are, taken by themselves. It was rather the *moral* lessons that the development of logic and metalogic seemed to teach. I say this despite the fact that in my work in philosophy on the whole I have devoted almost no time to the systematic investigation of ethical problems or principles. I might try to put the moral of modern symbolic logic as I understand it, beginning with Boole, Frege, Peano, Russell, Wittgenstein, Tarski, Carnap and Quine, among others, in this very general way. When we try to have everything we want in logic or in life, we usually pay an unexpected price for it somewhere later down the line. This seemed to be the fate of the most ambitious formal symbolic logics, of logicism, and of such projects as Hilbert's program in meta-mathematics. All of these efforts, despite their first bright promise and intuitive sense of rightness, have turned out to be limited in their pretensions by logic's own symbolic devices as revealed in a variety of syntactical, semantic, and set-theoretical diagonalizations.

Logic as such offers a moral parable for all of life. It is not until the full consequences of what we have set in motion by undertaking an action or adopting an axiom in a formal system become clear that the world or logic itself can come crashing down on our most naively cherished aspirations. Another moral caution, if that is the right word, that I sensed might be derived from the history and contemporary practice of logic, is that we can expect as a rule to be tested by exceptions that are typically owing to some individual other than the system's author or development team who, from the outside, so to speak, reveals a logical system's transgression of unanticipated limitations. As logicians working toward systematization, we are often too close to our own work to appreciate a formalism's faults, and our focus is usually on the positive results we hope the logic will enable us to attain. We are then often misled by our intuitions about whether or not a given set of axioms and inference rules is, for example, syntactically consistent and deductively complete and compact. There again we find a moral for those looking to generalize from the journey modern logic has taken to other areas of human endeavor, and a choice of inferences about the perils to avoid if we want to maximize the soundness and significance of a preferred system of logic in light of the hazards to which it may turn out in due course to be subject. The ancient Greeks mythologized this kind of general interplay as the pursuit of hubris by Nemesis. The analogy is by no means perfect, since it seems inaccurate to characterize the giants of logic as hubristic. They were understandably enthusiastic about their projects and unaware of the difficulties entailed by their positing of definitions, axioms and rules of inference that falsely seemed to offer safe ground for logical inference.

Frege is brought up short by Russell. Russell by Wittgenstein and Gödel, and Frege, Russell and Wittgenstein by Gödel. If Gödel has not yet been brought up short it is partly because he made his mark in logic by limiting logical constructions rather than advancing logical constructions of his own. By this I do not mean to downplay either the importance of the discovery of Gödel's metatheorems, nor his later writings in logic, including the independence of the continuum hypothesis from the axioms of standard Zermelo-Fraenkel set theory. Another moral to be gleaned from logic's rich history is that we must also sometimes learn to be more patient about these kinds of things. Gödel's proof is enjoying its day, but it too has limitations. These are explicit but not always heeded, and they determine the extent to which we as logicians can draw further philosophical implications from the deductive incompleteness of a syntactically consistent first-order predicate-quantificational logic with sufficient expressive capability to represent the axioms of an infinitary arithmetic, and in particular with recursive operators for addition and multiplication and an identity relation. Similar remarks apply also to Church's theorem, in which some of the explicit requirements in Gödel's first metatheorem are relaxed, but others, such as the concept of a finite extension, however useful and intuitive, are introduced. Each such commitment raises the philosophical possibility of forestalling limiting metatheorems by introducing and enforcing distinctions, objections to stipulations on which the theorems are founded, or striking out formally in new and potentially more fruitful and insightful directions. There seems to be a duality between diagonalizations or self-non-applicational constructions on the one hand and infinite regresses on the other. We see this in the liar and its solution in an infinitely regressive Tarskian hierarchy of object and meta-languages, in Russell's infinitely regressive type theory hierarchy and Gödel's dilemmatic self-non-applicational diagonalization, and even, among many others, in Plato's infinitely regressive Third Man and Aristotle's self-non-applicational inherence metaphysics of secondary in primary substances. In the aftermath of the discovery of limiting metatheorems, should we feel secure again in our work, provided we observe the boundaries established by these results? That, I think, would also be to ignore the sobering lessons of logic's past.[1]

It is moral principles such as these found everywhere in the history of logic and metalogic that have fueled much of my interest in symbolic logic. I am intrigued by the dialectic or back and forth movement in the development of logic that has yet to produce a crisis that has not resulted in improvement and refinement. Logic in one sense is the most rarified of disciplines, possessed of the greatest generality and expected to justify inference in all reasoning. There is nevertheless always a human drama behind the scenes in the rise and fall of logical systems, and its history edifyingly illustrates limits that may apply in the abstract to all human aspirations. What would we like to have in logic? An unrestricted extensional comprehension principle like Basic Law V in Frege's *Grundgesetze der Arithmetik*? A rigorous proof, as David Hilbert hoped, of every true proposition forthcoming from within the rigorously formalized syntax of a mathematical language? There are good positive reasons for embracing such expectations about the potentialities of formal logics. We must try our best to achieve them, and then pick up the pieces and put them together in a new more sophisticated or at least more fully informed way than we had previously attempted when we fail. In logic, again as in life

---

[1] I take the opportunity here to hazard an interpretation concerning Gödel's 1931 metatheorems. I have often thought that Gödel's original aim in arithmetizing the syntax of classical first-order logic in *Principia Mathematica* was simply to find a way of circumventing type-theory restrictions in order to resurrect a straightforward diagonalization like the liar sentence. Denying the provability of a formula as systematically coded by a natural number does not involve the attachment of a syntax item of a given type to another syntax item of the same type. When the tactic did not entirely succeed as intended, Gödel in the process may then have discovered the famous deductive completeness versus syntactical consistency dilemma enshrined in the first 1931 theorem as an equally if not more interesting implication of his argument. If this suggestion is correct as an insight into his efforts, then Gödel at the outset may have been striving for an outright contradiction in *Principia*, similar to the liar but tailored to avoid the logic's restrictions on syntax types. It is only when a syntactical inconsistency as such was not forthcoming in the second half of the proof that Gödel serendipitously recognized the implication of a forced choice between consistency and completeness. If any reader knows of documentation to support or refute this conjecture, I would greatly appreciate the information.

outside the formal disciplines, we are compelled to do so. Logic itself in due course nevertheless teaches that we cannot have all these amenities unless we are prepared to accept logical inconsistencies. Nor can we assume that paraconsistent logics will provide a panacea for all of the problems we can get ourselves into with unrestricted comprehension, among other naïve logical desiderata. It rather depends in every instance on where exactly the inconsistencies occur in a formalism, threatening its semantic integrity from within or without, and whether or not we can tolerate them theoretically even when classical inferential explosion is contained. We eventually learn cruel and interesting limitations in symbolic logic. Part of the excitement is that the field after so many harvests is still inexhaustibly abundant. In their most general terms, precisely because they are so abstract, the deeply moral lessons of symbolic logic are even more interesting and archetypal than the counterpart limitations we encounter more generally in everyday life.

What example(s) from your work illustrates the role formal methods can play in philosophy?

I have worked both as system builder and critic of logical systems. My projects in logic have largely centered on efforts to do justice, first, to the semantics of the true or false sentences of natural science, and in the second instance on extrascientific uses of formal and colloquial languages. Roughly, I began as a Quinean, graduated to Davidsonianism, and ended up throughout most of my career and at the current time of writing as an unregenerate but revisionary Meinongian. This, needless to say, has been a conscientious rather than market-savvy series of transitions, given the current logical and philosophical institutional scene.

My first logical system-building involved intensional systems intended to support the reference and true predication of constitutive properties to any and all objects regardless of their ontic status. The purpose was to provide a more general intuitive semantics for the truth values of propositions ostensibly about nonexistent entities, including law-governed idealizations, in the language of natural science, that would also do duty for predications in fiction, practical reasoning, and discourse outside of science, than was available in standard extensionalist logics and semantics, inspired (and arguably straitjacketed) especially by the partial success of what F.P. Ramsey designated as 'that paradigm of philosophy', Russell's theory of definite descriptions. Here the task was to adapt the notation of standard logic, in part to determine how far and in what directions it could be stretched, to suit the purposes of an ontically agnostic logic to which a semantics with both an extensional and extra-extensional component could productively be attached. The ease with which this was capable of being done, despite the need to overcome certain technical obstacles, and the satisfying fit of the interpretation, satisfaction and truth conditions that the logic made possible, provides yet another example of the moral dimensions of philosophical logic. The extraordinary animus with which extensionalism has been defended and the proponents of alternative semantics have been criticized or ignored reveals an aspect of the seemingly impersonal mechanical side of logic that should remind philosophers once again that, whatever we may choose to say about logic as such, if only we can satisfy ourselves that we have finally arrived at correct symbolizations, the discovery and elaboration and philosophical thinking surrounding the construction of formal systems of symbolic logic is after all very much a human endeavor with all of the same kinds of elements that characterize human culture in science, art, architecture, music, politics, or religion.

I have also been engaged over the years in criticisms of received logical systems and more especially of key assumptions about the nature of widely discussed paradoxes, puzzles, and limitations in logic. It has been my fate in considering the logical paradoxes to be largely unimpressed by paradoxes that have attracted the attention of commentators and engendered the most ingenious solutions. These prominently include the liar, Russell, Curry and other paradoxes. As a reflection of my deeply ingrained contrarianism – I have been like this for as long as I can remember – I have been far more concerned about less respected problems like Grelling's paradox, and the Pseudo-Scotus or validity paradox, including my own variation of the inference, which I have dubbed the soundness paradox. From a philosophical perspective, I find it natural to regard paradoxes as conceptual challenges to be overcome, rather than ultimate threats to logical consistency. If there were genuine logical paradoxes, then the universe we inhabit would not be a logical possible world. I never expect, although I have no conclusive reason to deny, that all paradoxes might surrender to the same general style of solution. Instead, I consider each according to its own terms and the special problems it raises. If a paradox interests me, I try to solve it if at all possible by specific but usually very pedestrian methods of identifying equivocations or imposing intuitively plausible restrictions on certain distinctions, or by uncovering other errors of reasoning that have contributed to the mistaken judgment that a genuine paradox needs to be solved. Afterwards, we can sometimes gather these distinctions and insights together and try to weave them into the fabric of beliefs, practical judgments, and theoretical, especially scientific, conclusions that we have independently reached. I think that many of these kinds of solutions can be knit together into distinct families of approaches, suggesting in most cases that the apparent paradoxes themselves belong to corresponding families in which logical or conceptual blunders of different sorts are being made.

In this regard, aside from my accidental use of the term 'family' in this connection, I suppose that my policy toward the paradoxes has been most profoundly influenced by Wittgenstein in both his early and later periods. The methods I have found most expedient for deflating the standard paradoxes have nevertheless virtually nothing to do with Wittgenstein's logical atomism, picture theory of meaning, or general form of proposition, nor, except in the most general terms that I think most Wittgensteinians would be quick to join me in disowning, with Wittgenstein's later appeal to philosophical grammar as a kind of therapy in which paradoxes among other traditional philosophical problems can be psychologically overcome in the sense of being quieted at least in their urgency. I insist whenever possible on using the most widely accepted methods of logic to uncover errors in ordinary logic. When I cannot find such internal solutions, I consider the problem at least temporarily unsolved, and, like the problem of whether dinosaurs were warm-blooded or cold-blooded, possibly one that in the course of human history will never be satisfactorily decided. Ideally, I want logic to cure itself, or to take care of itself, in Wittgenstein's arresting watchwords in both the *Tractatus Logico-Philosophicus* and *Notebooks 1914–1916*. This is the more profound, and I venture to say perhaps truer, Wittgensteinian sense of the scope and limits of logic with which I confront the paradoxes.

As a further indication of my interest and work in formal systems, I should probably use the present occasion to sound off against some of cynicism I have heard from colleague logicians. It has become fashionable to hold that logic students do not learn more from the experience than how to do logic, and in particular that they do not learn how to reason or think or write more competently. My experience is different. I have been led to conclude that logic courses, for students who are sufficiently well-motivated to learn what an introductory exposure to basic logical techniques has to offer, do in fact profit from their study. I tell my students playfully that studying logic will recondition their synapses in beneficial ways, but I am prepared unscientifically to believe that something like this is in fact true of longterm exposure to work. Whatever the success different instructors may have in teaching logic, I am persuaded that formalization in logic is often the best and sometimes the only route to understanding a philosophical or other conceptual problem or explicating a specimen of reasoning for purposes of critical evaluation. I also see moral and political advantages for a progressive free society in educating as many young decision-makers as possible in the methods of logical reasoning.

To better illustrate my use of formalization and faith in logical methods, I shall consider a concrete illustration from some of my recent unpublished doodling in logic. Here is an argument appearing in R.G. Collingwood's book, *An Autobiography*, in which Collingwood purports to refute metaphysical realism defined by John Cook Wilson as epistemic inefficacy. Wilson formulates the thesis as the incapacity of epistemic states to determine the properties of objects of knowledge. He explains realism accordingly as the view that 'knowing makes no difference to what is known'. Collingwood objects that any such formulation is 'meaningless' (p. 44). Collingwood originally presented the objection in a paper delivered to colleagues at Oxford University shortly after the end of WWII. He reasons as follows:

> I argued that any one who claimed, as Cook Wilson did, to be sure of this, was in effect claiming to know what he was simultaneously defining as unknown. For if you know that no difference is made to a thing θ by the presence or absence of a certain condition c, you know what θ is like with c, and also what θ is like without c, and on comparing the two find no difference. This involves knowing what θ is like without c; in the present case, knowing what you defined as unknown. (1939, with a new introduction by Stephen Toulmin. Oxford: The Clarendon Press, 1978, p. 44).

I am intrigued by this argument for several reasons. The inference seems plausible, but the conclusion is startling. I am often interested to see how many fundamental philosophical divisions appear to be unbridgeable and irreconcilable. This is especially true of such distinctions as rationalism v. empiricism, and their reverberations in other related areas of philosophy, such as the distinction between deontology v. consequentialism, extensionalism v. intensionalism, and, more to the immediate point, idealism v. realism. I was consulting Collingwood's *Autobiography* for entirely different reasons in preparing a lecture on his historiography for a Cambridge University meeting in 2006. I was trying to understand certain details of his dialectical 'logic' of question and answer with its non-Fregean presuppositional identity conditions for propositions. Collingwood proposes flatly to refute realism in favor of idealism on grounds that are supposed to be internal to realism itself. He offers to do something that I admire very much when it can be done. He wants to refute realism, so to speak, from out of realism's own mouth, on the basis of some of realism's most esteemed principles. The question as always is whether or not the argument actually works. If it does, as Collingwood seems not to have doubted, then its consequences can often be truly sweeping and revolutionary. To find out whether or not the disproof of metaphysical realism delivers its burden is quite another matter. Methods of symbolic logic, I optimistically believe, are among the best tools we have for deciding these controversies, and it was not long after reminding myself of Collingwood's stance that I began scribbling down translations of some of the key assumptions leading to his putative refutation of realism.

Collingwood describes a condition c of knowing a thing θ, which is such that, following Wilson's formula, 'makes no difference' to θ. This presumably means that θ remains the same regardless of whether $c\theta$ or $\neg c\theta$. Taken literally, the argument has something like the following logical form: Let $\tau(\theta)$ represent the totality of θ's properties, so that $\tau\theta = \{P_1, P_2, P_3, ...\}$, for some choice of properties $P_1, ..., P_n, ...$; let c represent the condition of something's being known, K propositional knowledge or knowing *that* something is the case, and R Wilsonian metaphysical realism. To say that knowing or not knowing θ makes no difference to θ in the sense of not making any difference to its properties, as Collingwood paraphrases Wilson's epistemic criterion for realism, might then be analyzed in this way:

1. $R \leftrightarrow \forall\theta\forall c\Diamond[c\theta \land \neg Kc\theta]$
2. $K\forall\theta\forall c\Diamond[c\theta \land \neg Kc\theta] \to K\forall\theta\forall c\exists\tau[[c\theta \to \tau\theta] \land [\neg c\theta \to \tau\theta]]$
3. $\forall\theta\forall c\neg\Diamond[c\theta \land \neg c\theta]$
4. $\forall\theta\forall c[\Diamond Kc\theta \leftrightarrow \Diamond K\neg c\theta]$

5. $\forall p[Kp \to p]$

6. $\forall p, q[K[p \to q] \to [Kp \to Kq]]$

7. $\forall p, q[\neg \Diamond p \to \neg \Diamond [p \wedge q]]$

---

8. $KR \to K\forall\theta\forall c \exists \tau[\neg c\theta \to \tau\theta]$

9. $[KR \to K\forall\theta\forall c \exists \tau[\neg c\theta \to \tau\theta]] \to [K\forall\theta\forall c \neg c\theta \to K\exists\tau\forall\theta\tau\theta]$

10. $K\exists\tau\forall\theta\tau\theta \to K\forall\theta\forall cc\theta$

11. $K\forall\theta\forall cc\theta \to \forall\theta\forall cc\theta$

12. $K\forall\theta\forall c \neg c\theta \to \forall\theta\forall c \neg c\theta$

13. $K\forall\theta\forall c \neg c\theta \to \forall\theta\forall c[c\theta \wedge \neg c\theta]$

14. $\forall\theta\forall c \neg \Diamond K \neg c\theta$

15. $\forall\theta\forall c \neg \Diamond Kc\theta$

16. $\forall\theta\forall c \neg \Diamond Kc\theta \to \forall\theta\forall c \neg \Diamond [c\theta \wedge \neg Kc\theta]$

17. $\forall\theta\forall c \neg \Diamond [c\theta \wedge \neg Kc\theta]$

18. $\neg R$

What I appreciate about this kind of formalization is its patient unpacking of a hidden complex logical structure. The reader can work out the translation and interpolate the justifications for each step in standard logic.

To symbolize the argument took me about 7 continuous hours after the third or fourth frustrating day of trying to make headway with Collingwood's reasoning. In a logical reconstruction, I believe that the work of analysis should be borne by formalizations of relations essential to an author's thought. Logical relations linking proposition to proposition, on the other hand, should ideally involve only bivalent first-order propositional and predicate-quantificational logic, the weakest modal system, and, relative to these logics, the fewest possible extra-logically defined predicates (in this case, an epistemic operator), regardless of how the semantics of these languages are explained and formalized.

That is what I generally strive for in my first efforts to work out the formalization of a piece of discourse like Collingwood's argument. If and when these efforts prove futile, and I absolutely must turn to something nonclassical or even invent something for the occasion, I do so reluctantly and usually with the attitude that I am proceeding only provisionally and hypothetically, to make at least some progress in better understanding the concepts and relations I am trying to interpret. Here, too, I prefer whenever possible to work as conservatively as possible until the subject matter requires something more adventurous, so that every departure from classical systems is justified in my mind as demanded by the argument's concepts and relations themselves.

During much of the time it took me to devise the above translation (which I naturally consider to be only provisional and capable of being refined), I was simply stuck, and often reduced to scrawling or staring out into space. I was unable for a long time to penetrate Collingwood's compact prose to arrive at a satisfactory charitable symbolization. I wanted as always to give the argument the best possible run for its money. If there is a way to make an author's thinking deductively valid, I do my best to try to find it, because I think that there is no better way to understand what the author is saying. This, indeed, is how I generally interpret and try to implement the principle of charity. I view the work of symbolization as an opportunity to clarify the content and logical structure of an argument. An argument that I select for analysis will typically be one that fascinates or concerns me or that I perceive as an interesting challenge to try to formalize. This was certainly my experience in working with Collingwood's objection to Wilsonian metaphysical realism.

The problem in this case was understanding exactly what the argument is trying to say. I did all of the usual things in trying to recover meaning from a text, repeating the crux of the argument multiple times, slowly, out loud, fixing my attention on how my first grasp of the meaning of the sentences and how they appear to relate logically to one another before trying formally to symbolize the argument's assumptions and conclusions. Throughout much of this process, I was unsatisfied that I understood exactly what Collingwood was saying, so I began to translate the most basic components of the passage into logical symbolism. Clearly, the argument was supposed to be some sort of *reductio ad absurdum* of Wilsonian metaphysical realism. The immediate questions I wanted to consider were: What is Wilson's epistemic criterion of metaphysical realism (beyond the intuitive content of the colloquial formulation that the act of knowing makes no difference to what is known or to the intended object of knowledge)? How should Wilson's concept of metaphysical realism be formalized? The answer to this question was vital to understanding the argument, because Collingwood claims that Wilson's concept upon analysis is logically incoherent. Thus, everything rides on getting Wilson right, at least by capturing the sense Collingwood seems to attribute to him as the basis for his criticism.

I experimented with a variety of formulations. In the end, I thought it was important to represent Wilsonian realism as R is defined above, logically equivalent to the thesis, adopting Collingwood's choice of terms, that for any thing θ and any condition c (read property, quality or relation), it is logically possible for the object to have the condition but for it not to be (impersonally) known, K, that the object has the condition. I was relatively happy with this because it represents what I regard as essential to Wilson's realism—that there can be more to the world than any thinking subject happens to know. Collingwood does not speak in terms of alethic logically possibility as such, but my sense was that what he says might be open to this interpretation. Moving provisionally, once I thought I had adequately formalized Wilson's thesis, my purpose was to test the body of Collingwood's objection against the argument. If the argument worked well in exposing a hidden contradiction in Wilson's realism, then the definition could be supported to that extent at least as a plausible formalization of Collingwood's target if not of Wilson's own exact view. If the argument failed against such an analysis, then I would reap two gains. First, I would have justification for rethinking and possibly modifying the definition of Wilsonian realism as the focus of a charitable interpretation of Collingwood's objection. Second, as a result, I would have in hand the basis for criticizing Collingwood's objection as directed at something less than the most intuitively correct logical explication of Wilson's realism.

In the event, assuming the analysis is correct, the formalization of Wilsonian realism turned out to be essentially related to the formalization of Collingwood's *reductio*, in the sense that without something equivalent to this symbolization Collingwood could not produce the contradiction that finally appears in derivation step (13) from the intermediate conclusion that if Wilsonian realism is known to be true, then to know that a certain thing is unaffected by having or not having a given condition implies that it must be known what the thing is like both with and without the condition. Here, in application to Wilson's epistemic criterion for metaphysical realism, the problem is to *know* what a supposedly (possibly) *unknown* thing is like *both* when it is *known* and when it is *unknown*. The latter contradiction reflects back on the assumption that it is logically possible for any chosen thing to have (in reality) a property that it is not known to have in the thought or epistemic state of any thinking subject. All of these essential features are made explicit in the formalization. The crucial step for Collingwood appears in this symbolization at assumption (2), where the possibility of a thing's having a property outside the extent of all knowledge is further analyzed as there being a sum total of the thing's conditions other than it's being known (or unknown), which remains identical regardless of whether or not the thing has an otherwise arbitrary condition. It is clearly this implication of Wilsonian realism that Collingwood regards as incoherent. An adequate charitable formalization of Collingwood's reasoning must therefore try to symbolize this part of his objection as correctly exposing a logical inconsistency in Wilson's epistemic slogan for metaphysical realism, according to which the act of knowing makes no difference to what is known.

To produce a clearcut contradiction that reflects on the original definition of Wilsonian realism is a back and forth process. It is a matter of working with preferred notations and assumptions so as eventually to reveal a basis for inconsistency that derives from the definitions and assumptions by which things are said to have whatever (other) conditions they have independently of whether their conditions (other than being known or unknown) are known or not known. The *reductio* is accordingly reconstructed in a series of steps that lay out each move of elementary deductive logic leading to the negation of the definition of Wilsonian realism. The contradiction arises for any thing when to know that the definition of metaphysical realism itself is true, as Collingwood argues, is to know what a hypothetically unknown thing is like were it precisely to lack in particular the condition of being known.

When the analysis of Collingwood's objection after many false trials at last lays all these essential features of the argument open to view in a deductively valid logically structure that is classical, minimally modal and trades only on widely accepted principles of epistemic logic, or, indeed, of the concept of knowledge, then I can be satisfied that I have arrived at a viable if not absolutely final unimprovable formalization. The fact that I am in a position now to say informally what I believe Collingwood's argument to hold is in turn a product of the back and forth process of formal interpretation. My understanding of the argument and its components are checked and updated against the evolving formalism, and the formalism was in turn frequently checked against my evolving intuitive sense of the argument's structure and content. If the symbolization succeeds, or to the extent that it may seem to do so, the result is generally owing to the dialogue that I think must always take place between colloquial discourse and its symbolic logical formalization. I think there is such a thing as getting an argument right when translating it into a logical notation, although there are often different purposes that require different levels of penetration of logical analysis of the content and relation of an inference's assumptions and conclusions.

The principal motivation for undertaking formalization of arguments in colloquial discourse is to understand more exactly what they are saying. A further crucial part of this process is to turn back to the symbolization when it seems to be complete and everything seems to snap properly into place as a basis for criticism. Collingwood's argument is remarkable because it proposes to refute (Wilsonian) metaphysical realism defined as epistemic inefficacy on purely logical grounds. Does his reasoning, once we believe we have correctly reconstructed it, actually uncover a logical inconsistency in this seemingly intuitive epistemic formulation of metaphysical realism? The second, complementary, main reason why I like the above symbolization of the argument is that it facilitates criticism by inviting a closer inspection of the assumptions and conclusions of the inference, focusing on specific parts of the reasoning that would otherwise be more difficult if not impossible to examine with the same degree of concentration.

The interpretive process, as already indicated must not end here. It is usually not enough to produce a decisive conclusion that Collingwood's argument succeeds or fails, even if good reasons for either of these conclusions are provided. It remains always a possibility if the argument fails or succeeds for what appear to be the wrong reasons that the fault lies with the formalization rather than with the author's thinking, and it may therefore be necessary to engage in additional refinement, in light of whatever criticisms the argument as formalized proves heir to or immune from, in order to make sure that we are working all along with an accurate translation into formal symbolism. My criticism of Collingwood's argument must await another occasion, but the interested reader is encouraged to look more closely at the unrestricted (higher-order) quantification over conditions in both the definition of R in assumption (1) and in its Collingwood-inspired explication in assumption (2), and to ask exactly how these assumptions would minimally need to be qualified in order to prevent the inference especially in derivation step (10) from going through.

What is the proper role of philosophy in relation to other disciplines?

The question of how philosophy relates to other subjects suggests a transcendental perspective, as though we could look at philosophy from outside its practice and independently of any first-level philosophical assumptions. This, I think, is an untenable proposition. A complete philosophy must specify its relation to other disciplines, and it is only in this sense that I can try to say how I see my own philosophical outlook standing in relation to other disciplines. The relation is complicated, not only in its details, but in the fact that I approve philosophical principles in part on the basis of how they will ultimately collectively stand in relation to beliefs and practices in the other arts and sciences.

Old-fashioned as it may appear, I regard philosophy as investigating the meaningfulness of the questions and propositions entertained in all theorizing, including philosophy. This investigation takes many forms. It includes philosophical semantics and hence ontology and philosophy of mind, and in particular metaphysics. Logic is the expressive schematization and inferential modeling of all reasoning, including logic and philosophy. I think the latter is true, in particular, regardless of how logic and philosophy themselves turn out to be related. My view is that logic as the formal structure of all reasoning governs all aspects of theorization in all fields, with the exception, if we exclude as a special case formal ontology and whatever else might be juiced from the metaphysical commitments embedded in logical symbolisms, of a theory's most basic concepts and principles. If this is true, then it follows that we cannot get away from logic or consider other disciplines independently of logic in order to explain logic's relation to them. By analogy, I would say that the study of logic is something like opthamology. Logic is presupposed by any investigation, as a normally functioning eye is presupposed by any visual empirical inquiry. This does not preclude using logic to study logic, just as there is no profound difficulty in using one's eyes to study the structure and function of the eye. The only catch is that in both cases a certain distance or mechanical reflection is required involving the eye or logic alternatively as subject and object. We need a mirror, in effect, or a relay of cameras, that enables the eye to see itself; analogically, we need a representation of logic within its own syntax by special referential conventions, so that it can also serve not only as the object of study but the medium through which it is studied. The greater risk in the case of logic, methodologically speaking, is that our understanding of logic is more likely to be distorted, perhaps inevitably so, when viewed through the lens of a particular preferred logic. If it is true that all disciplines presuppose logic and depend on logic as the structure of reasoning for their conclusions, then logic in some sense presupposes itself. I know many logicians and epistemologists who are not troubled in the least by this situation, but I think that efforts must be made to avoid circularity in the conclusions we draw about the nature and scope and limits of logic in light of this peculiar interdependence.

Of course, we might imagine that there is an Ur-Logik or primitive logic, on which we rely when we fashion formal systems of logic. Unfortunately, this proposal gives too prominent a role to such innate principles of inference in comparison with the logics that have been developed with their aid, and exempts them from articulation and formalization. This is unsatisfactory, if for no other reason, then because many if not most logicians conceive of their work as precisely that of trying to spell out in a mathematical language the most basic principles of reasoning that we are imagining to constitute the Ur-Logik. In any case, why should there be any unformalizable logic? Why in particular should the most fundamental principles of correct reasoning not be capable of exact expression? If we attempt to formalize them, on the other hand, then we are back to the original problem of our commitment to a particular logic coloring our use of formal methods to understand logic generally. I tentatively think that the problem is real and that the best solution is to adopt a floating perspective, in which we develop all logical formalisms to the greatest extent possible and view each in turn from the standpoint of the others. We can consider the strengths and limitations of a paraconsistent logic from the standpoint of Boolean algebra, and we can consider the strengths and limitations of standard first-order logic from the standpoint of relevance logic, of relevance logic from the standpoint of standard first-order logic, and the like. None of this precludes logicians from favoring one system over another as preferable for a particular set of analytic tasks, or from regarding one or another of these systems as the best, most correct, or ultimately true system of logic. Nor does it require logicians to adopt any of these controversial perspectives. The discovery or design of such a logic can then be understood as the formalization of the inchoate principles of logic that have guided its development, if only in groping fashion, until it has reached such a point of clarification in mathematical expression that it can be compared with its competitors and assessed from a variety of standpoints for its advantages and disadvantages. Whether or not this conclusion is finally correct, it positively reflects the kinds of experience I have had in logical system building and in formalizing pre-symbolic logical reasoning, such as that contained in Collingwood's alleged refutation of metaphysical realism.

Alternatively, I think it is intelligible also to regard the proliferation of logical systems in what I have elsewhere recently referred to as 'the logic candy store' as different facets of a single underlying logic that has yet to be fully explicated as something common to them all. At time of writing, on the other hand, my own judgment is that so far no particular system of logic has emerged as clearly superior to all rivals, and certainly no underlying universal logic common to the plethora of formal systems currently available and championed by their proponents has been identified. The temptation that I share with other logicians is to want to say that despite their differences all of these systems are logics, and that in working with any of them we are in some general sense doing logic. It may nevertheless be true that we are dealing here with what the later Wittgenstein refers to as a family resemblance concept, and that alternative systems of logic have in common only the fact that they are all efforts to formalize different principles of reasoning, each appropriate to a different subject matter, just as Euclidean and non-Euclidean geometries all have in common only the fact that they are efforts to mathematicize different conceptions of space. I think that this is in many ways a satisfactory way out of at least some of the problems in understanding the nature of logic, but it does not immediately lay to rest the nagging sense that there must nevertheless be a higher or more general universal logic. I am struck by the fact that so many logicians and philosophers historically have had this same conviction that logic is somehow an exception and that the wide variety of logics may yet be integrated into a single formal system that would deserve to be called logic or *the* logic, without qualification.

It seems eminently reasonable also to wonder whether our conceptual scheme, if such a unitary thing exists, can possibly be coherent if different mutually incompatible and jointly inconsistent logics are in fact required as the most appropriate formalizations of the range of distinct concepts that happen to characterize human thought. I consider this to be a central problem for the future in philosophy of logic, which leads directly to the following question.

What do you consider the most neglected topics and/or contributions in late 20th century philosophy?

Here is a short but hopefully suggestive list, some items of which have enjoyed more lively philosophical discussion in the past but have been set aside in favor of other recent preoccupations. I do not maintain that these topics are neglected in the sense that they have been utterly ignored or discouraged by recent and contemporary philosophers and logicians, but only by virtue of their not being given sufficient or in any case the right kind of attention that I think they deserve.

- The concept of infinity.
- The relation between language, art, and other artifacts.
- The relation between intension and extension.
- The unity or disunity of logic(s) and the implications of this for understanding human conceptualization and cognition.
- The relation between intentionality and qualia.
- The duality between self-non-application (diagonalization) and infinite regress.
- The role of significance in the evaluation of arguments.
- Heuristics of purpose in logical and mathematical discovery.
- Aesthetics of logic and mathematics.
- The implications of paraphrasis in ontic reduction.
- Meinong's object theory.
- Schopenhauer's critique of logical formalisms in abstract versus intuitive knowledge.
- Conditional intent.
- The concept of potentiality.

- Metaphysics of agency.
- Ontology and epistemology of applied mathematics.
- Prospects for an Aristotelian inherence ontology of mathematical entities.
- Circularity in definition and argument.
- Why there is something rather than nothing.
- Whether and if so why there is exactly one logically contingent actual world.
- Logical and mathematical concepts in relation to religious attitudes.
- Friendship and the good life.

What are the most important open problems in philosophy and what are the prospects for progress?

In some sense, I consider all philosophical problems to be open. Otherwise they wouldn't be (a) philosophical or (b) problems. This is not to say that I have not provisionally made up my mind about some of them, or that I'm not prepared to argue with some vigor about the conclusions I have reached.

Although I have devoted much time to reading and thinking about Wittgenstein's (anti-) philosophy, there are many areas where I am conscious of disagreeing with Wittgenstein emphatically on what I think are grounds that ought to have convinced him also. An immediate case in point is Wittgenstein's remark that we are to attain conceptual clarity in order to achieve therapeutic peace of mind from nagging philosophical problems. This notion of therapy is entirely alien to my way of thinking, which celebrates instead an irrepressible productive anxiety. What I would say instead is that conceptual clarity is a relative value to be approached only in the process of working with and finding our way into, around and through philosophical problems. Thus, I see in philosophical problems, both putative and genuine, including logical problems, an essential part of the cure for rather than a cause or symptom of some sort of literal or metaphorical disease of conceptual confusion. The remedy, where such is demanded, is effected to whatever extent this proves possible by struggling with philosophical problems and not implausibly supposing that philosophical problems can ever be generally or globally set aside as spurious.

For example, I do not consider the mind-body problem to be still open, but satisfactorily solved by a form of property dualism in which the intentional properties of thought and its qualia are distinguished from purely physical properties of the brain and neuro-system. In contrast, I have no clue whatsoever as to the morality of such actions within human choice as abortion and euthanasia. I think I know what I personally would or would not do in such situations, and what I would or would not want to have happen to me if I were a candidate for certain of these actions, but I do not have the first idea of how a philosopher ought to set about trying to justify any of the answers that an ethicist might propose in facing up to real life practical dilemmas. Many of my reactions to longstanding problems in logic and mathematics on the other hand are certain to seem facile to certain critics. As an empiricist I want to avoid any argumentation in the formal disciplines that presupposes the logical possibility or more generally the intelligibility of the concept of infinity. By withdrawing the welcome mat to infinite sets and series in logic and mathematics we cut the ground from under Gödel, Church, Cantor, Löwenheim-Skolem, Lindström, the Turing halting problem, and many another inconvenience to the real-time uses of symbolic logic to which we finite creatures pragmatically considered are inherently limited. By resisting the force of the liar paradox and other logical, semantic, and set theoretical diagonalizations, logic is freed within its limits to shrug off the motivations for an infinite Tarskian hierarchy of languages and metalanguages. Likewise, by paying careful attention to concealed equivocations among the assumptions and conclusions of many improperly articulated arguments, it is possible to refute other challenges from within logic to the integrity of much of the most endearing naïve parts of logic. Why, after all, should we fret over the mapping of domains with infinite cardinalities when we seem to have no clear idea of transfinite sets and series independently of the notations by which we purport to refer to them? Why, if such assumptions saddle us with avoidable logical problems and theoretical gaps, should we insist on admitting them to the ontology? We should include them only if we cannot properly transact the business of pure or applied mathematics without them, but this is a very doubtful assumption in the case of infinities and higher infinite cardinals and orders of infinity.

I am inclined to cut the Gordean knot precisely here. As a result, I find myself largely in sympathy with strict finitists, including those intuitionists who reject infinite and transfinite sets and series on conscientious epistemic or other cognitive or pragmatic grounds. (I exclude L.E.J. Brouwer, whose metaphysics of mathematics and its logic as created by thought is more subtle than the epistemic scruples that are sometimes invoked for limiting standard principles of logic.) Naturally, this kind of decisive undermining of many of the most interesting results of twentieth century logic is often met not only with skepticism and hostility, but incredulity. How can one hope to sustain such a naïve strictly finitist formulation of logic? I can only reply that I do not love logical problems for their own sake, and that my own aesthetic sense of the capabilities of logic and its role in thought is such as to recommend the simplest and ontically least profligate referential domain needed to support the kinds of logical reasoning finite reasoning creatures such as ourselves actually need and can actually comprehend, whose implications they can actually put to use in the most ontically demanding theoretical and practical inferences that do not simply presuppose the existence of infinite sets and series.

Let the question, then, of whether or not infinite sets or series should be countenanced in the philosophy of logic and mathematics serve as a good example of what I take to be an open philosophical problem. It is a large problem as judged by its consequences for our understanding not only of logic but of the physical world and its dimensions, and of such methodological divisions as that between a priorism and a posteriorism. Many different kinds of philosophical commitments are similarly linked together in a more comprehensive network of explicit assumptions and implicit presuppositions that can often be traced back to deeply fundamental ideologies underlying the philosophy of logic and mathematics. I consider the problem to be philosophical because it is a clearly conceptual matter that I do not expect science or history or any other discipline outside of philosophy to be able to address. I consider the problem to be open because while I admire the formalizations of infinitary and transfinitary logic and mathematics for their beauty and expansion of domains beyond the limits of imaginability, I do not share with equal enthusiasm the prospects of their being reconciled to objections about whether or not we can have clear ideas of such things, and, if not, of whether we have any business introducing higher-order cardinals and ordinals to the formal disciplines. I do not know of a conclusive objection to such profligate ontologizing in logic and mathematics, but I find myself inclined to reject infinity solely on the grounds that we do not really need or use it except within the industry that talk about infinity has itself created. We jettison many of the most stubborn and annoying paradoxes and limitations in logical theory and metatheory by restricting logic and mathematics to finite domains of unpredetermined cardinality, including those generated by intuitionistic choice sequences. I think I know my own instincts clearly, and I have offered a number of arguments in their support, but it is quite another thing to have in hand a knockdown philosophical argument against infinite sets and series.

As to the prospects for success in solving any of these outstanding logic-related philosophical problems, I think that they are probably about the same as they have ever been.

10

Mark Jago

Lecturer
Department of Philosophy
University of Nottingham, UK

Why were you initially drawn to formal methods?

I was drawn to formal philosophy almost by accident. As a philosophy undergraduate, I had become frustrated by the lack of answers on offer. As I began studying logic, I was hopeful that the topic would be the one to shed light on the problems I had encountered in my epistemology and metaphysics courses. Logic provides a precise way of formulating a problem and exact reasoning techniques. Hidden assumptions that can often pass unnoticed when an argument is given informally in English have to be made explicit in the formal version of the argument.

It soon became apparent to me, however, that the most interesting logical results, on the course I was taking at least, were negative results. As is common in philosophy, 'logic' was taken to mean 'classical first-order logic.' The first blow was learning that first-order logic is undecidable. We have a way of testing whether an argument is valid or not but the procedure we use is not guaranteed to halt after any finite length of time. So first-order logic cannot be looked at as a completely automated way of solving problems.

The next blow was learning of the expressive limitations of first-order logic. I cannot say, for example, that Napoleon was not one of my ancestors in first-order logic. An ancestor is a parent, or one of their parents, or one of their parents, and so on; it is this 'and so on' that we cannot express in first-order logic. To express the *ancestor* relation, second-order logic is needed, in which we can quantify over groups of individuals as well as over the individuals themselves. The problem is that we cannot write down rules for producing all the true sentences of second-order logic. One cannot even define what we mean by 'natural number' in first-order logic (in a way that rules out 'rogue' elements that we don't want to count as natural numbers) and so even the seemingly simple area of basic arithmetic seemed beyond the scope of logic. In short, the prospects of using logical techniques to solve philosophical disputes looked bleak to me. I had trouble seeing how progress in philosophy could be made by anyone, let alone by me!

After completing my BA, I decided to take a PhD in theoretical computer science. I knew relatively little about the area except that it was moving along at a frightening speed. I found that there were many interesting avenues in logical research that I had previously been unaware of. In particular, there was complexity theory, which doesn't just ask whether our test for the validity of an argument will terminate with an answer but also asks, just how much time is needed to give an answer? and how much space (i.e. memory) does the test need to run?

Logic became exciting once again, partly because of a much broader conception of what constitutes logic. There were modal logics, constructive logics, type-theoretical logics, substructural logics, fuzzy logics, paraconsistent logics; the list went on and on. I took an interest in modal logics, which combine two very handy features. Firstly, they are often robustly decidable, so that our tests for validity always return an answer in a finite time. But they are also extremely useful in computer science and artificial intelligence. They can be used to model change in dynamic systems, the knowledge of artificial agents or the behaviour of computer programs, for example; they can also be combined to model all of these things at once.

However, I had one nagging worry. Questions that seemed fundamental to theoretical computer science were, from my perspective, being overlooked. I would often hear how classical logic (which assumes that, for any proposition p, either p or its negation $\neg p$ must be true) is utterly meaningless. Constructive (or intuitionistic) logic was preferred in its place, because the proofs built in this logic can be thought of as computer programs. In particular, constructive natural deduction proofs correspond to the simply-typed lambda calculus, which forms the basis of the function approach to programming languages. But I could never get a satisfactory explanation of why classical logic is completely meaningless, other than 'my computer can't understand it'. It seemed at least possible that *we* understand it.

Deep questions about meaning, even in the domain of logic and theoretical computer science, are philosophical in nature and call for a philosophical rather than purely logical approach. I didn't want to shy away from these philosophical questions but I wanted to make use of the formal tools that I had learnt. Luckily for me, it was around this time that I discovered that there was an entire community applying formal techniques to philosophical problems.

What example(s) from your work illustrates the role formal methods can play in philosophy?

At the beginning of my doctoral research, I began studying epistemic logics. As far as I was concerned, there was very little linking the logician's use of 'know' to the way it is used in epistemology. This did not seem acceptable to me. By way of example, many epistemic logics make use of possible-worlds semantics, which gives them the computational advantages of the modal logics I discussed above. The downside is that agents are said to know every logical consequence of what they know (this is known as the *logical omniscience problem*). As a consequence, if the sentence 'ϕ' is a logical truth, then every agent has to know it, automatically. This is clearly a strange idea. Many researchers have defended the idea and the many uses of epistemic logic in artificial intelligence and distributed computing show these logics to be invaluable; yet I could not help wonder whether a more realistic notion of knowledge could be accommodated.

In my PhD thesis, *Logics for Resource Bounded Agents*, I look at how realistic concepts of knowledge and belief can be incorporated within a logical framework. I start from a philosophical discussion of what belief is and develop a logic based on these considerations, the aim being to arrive at a logic that is just as useful to computer scientists as traditional epistemic logics but that has a secure philosophical basis and does not assume that agents are ideal logical reasoners. Any form of reasoning requires the reasoner to have certain abilities and to have enough time and memory to carry out the task. The formal approach that I develop combines the agent's belief states with possible ways for that agent to reason, given its abilities and the time and memory resources available, through which it can arrive at new belief states.

This formal work then sheds light on philosophical ideas, such as *epistemic possibility*. An epistemic possibility is supposed to be something that could be the case, for all I know. But there is a difficulty here: Does my knowledge rule out something's being an epistemic possibility if that thing is inconsistent with my knowledge? If so, then any contradictory hypothesis cannot be an epistemic possibility for any agent. Intuitively, this is not right: Mathematicians often take paradoxical hypotheses to be possible when they cannot spot the paradox because it is too deeply hidden. On my account, it is epistemically possible that p for an agent when the agent cannot produce an explicit contradiction between its knowledge and p (again, given the agent's abilities and resources available). What began as a look at a logical problem (logical omniscience) has metamorphosed into a philosophical account of belief and epistemic possibility, almost by chance.

There are many other areas of formal research that interact with (and hopefully shed light upon) philosophical areas. I will mention one more from formal epistemology. Epistemology is of course not just concerned with knowledge; justification is an important concept but one that has traditionally been lacking in the formal approach. Sergei Artemov realized that his work on the logic of proofs could be seen as adding a notion of justification to traditional epistemic logic. The idea is to label sentences by their justifications and then provide a calculus for combining justifications (see, for example, S. Artemov and E. Nogina, 'Introducing justification to epistemic logic,' *Journal of Logic and Computation* vol 15(6), pp. 1059-1073, 2005). In this example as well as in my own case, what began as research in logic has turned out to have applications to philosophical concepts, highlighting how formal methods have a role to play in epistemology.

What is the proper role of philosophy in relation to other disciplines?

I will restrict myself to considering the relation between philosophy and formal methods, including formal logic and mathematics. It is always possible to question the exact benefit of formal methods in philosophy. It is one thing to have a logic of justification or of epistemic possibility but just what does knowledge or justification itself consist in? In response to such 'what is ...?' questions, my feeling is that the response of the formal philosopher should be modest. In formal epistemology, for example, we should not expect a logic to reveal the nature of knowledge or justification itself. This was part of Hintikka's aim in his seminal *Knowledge and Belief: An Introduction to the Logic of Two Notions* in 1962.

Having given an account of knowledge and its accompanying logic, he notes that this notion is closed under logical consequence, i.e. we have the logical omniscience problem.

Hintikka's discussion up to this point had been couched in terms of consistency (for ϕ follows logically from a set of premises Γ in classical logic when $\Gamma \cup \neg\phi$ is inconsistent). Hintikka's initial response to the logical omniscience problem is to remark that the underlying notion of his logic is not really consistency at all but instead a notion of *defensibility*, relating to what it would be unwise to claim is false given prior knowledge. So claiming that I know that $p \wedge q$ but not p might be called consistent but it isn't defensible: I could be easily shown that p follows from what I say I know. However, we might reply to Hintikka that there isn't anything wrong with the notion of consistency in the logic; rather, the concept that is being modelled isn't knowledge!

It is notable that in the 44 years since Hintikka's book (which effectively began the area of formal epistemology) was published, despite the many advances in modal epistemic logic, the question, 'what is knowledge?' is still plagued by the Gettier cases. Responses on offer, such as contextualism, do not appeal overwhelmingly to formal techniques. These 'what is ...?' questions are inherently philosophical and I do not feel that they will be answered merely by applying formal techniques.

This is not to say that formal epistemology and formal philosophy in general cannot contribute to mainstream philosophy. There is more to philosophy than answering the 'what is ...?' questions! The area in which formal methods are most obviously of use in philosophy is the sharpening of our intuitions.

Let me give a good example of how this works in practice. Suppose you are an anti-realist about truth, who claims that it is meaningless to postulate unknowable truths. You claim that any truth whatsoever must be knowable, which we can write as

$$\forall p(p \rightarrow \Diamond \mathsf{K}p) \tag{10.1}$$

Here, we are quantifying over propositions (or declarative sentences, or statements) p. For the purposes of this example, '$\mathsf{K}p$' means that someone knows that p and so '$\Diamond \mathsf{K}p$' is read as, 'it is possible for someone to know that p.'

Now, just because you are an anti-realist does not mean that you think that all truths are actually known right now (which is clearly false). You only hold that they are *knowable*. So you agree that there are truths that are unknown at present:

$$\exists p(p \land \neg Kp) \tag{10.2}$$

Let us take 'p' to be an arbitrary unknown truth, so we have the following as an instance of (10.2):

$$p \land \neg Kp \tag{10.3}$$

Now we can substitute (10.3) into (10.1) to obtain:

$$(p \land \neg Kp) \rightarrow \Diamond K(p \land \neg Kp) \tag{10.4}$$

and by modus ponens from (10.4, 10.3) obtain

$$\Diamond K(p \land \neg Kp) \tag{10.5}$$

which states that it is possible to know that p is an unknowable truth. The problem is that, given a few reasonable assumptions, this just ain't the case. To see why not, suppose for the sake of argument that it is possible, i.e. that

$$K(p \land \neg Kp) \tag{10.6}$$

Now I point out that, if someone knows $(p \land \neg Kp)$, then

$$Kp \land K\neg Kp \tag{10.7}$$

That is, if someone knows the conjunction of two propositions, then she also knows each of those propositions on its own. Suppose you agree with me that this is so. I then point out that knowledge is *factive*: one can only know what is true, so if someone knows that p, then 'p' is true. But then, by applying factivity to the right conjunct '$K\neg Kp$', we have

$$Kp \land \neg Kp \tag{10.8}$$

which is a blatant contradiction: no one can both know that p and not know that p! Something has gone wrong here; (10.6) could not possibly be true. But (10.5) says that it is possible!

What this shows (using only simple natural deduction) is that we cannot hold all of these assumptions as true together. If you want to keep your thesis that all truths are knowable, you had better say that either knowledge is not factive, or else knowledge does not distribute over conjunction. This is a good example of a formal technique showing that certain assumptions rule out certain others, all of which sound plausible on their own. Given a little extra argument that knowledge is both factive and distributes over conjunction (which most philosophers would agree with), we have an argument against the anti-realist position.

The traditional problems of philosophy are not going to go away with the advent of new formal techniques, neither will the traditional methods of philosophy be supplanted. Rather, they will be augmented by new formal methods in a way that allows the existing arguments to be made more precisely and our intuitions on how to approach a topic to be sharpened. This means that, although mathematical techniques have a place in the philosophical method, philosophy is a discipline distinct from the mathematical sciences (and so from science in general).

What distinguishes philosophy is primarily its method. Above, I gave the example of the debate over constructive and non-constructive logics in theoretical computer science (a similar debate takes place in mathematics). The arguments evidently boil down to the meaning that these approaches to logic can be given but neither computer science nor mathematics itself has the resources to formulate these arguments in a wholly satisfactory way. Philosophical reasoning is required to advance either argument, which will be of a different style to the technical arguments that precede or follow it in the decision to adopt a particular approach to logic or mathematics.

What do you consider the most neglected topics and/or contributions in late 20th century philosophy?

It is hard in philosophy to discuss important but neglected areas because what we think of as philosophical topics (rather than, say, problems for linguistics or the physical or sociological sciences to work out) is dictated in a large part by prominent works of philosophy. Just what counts as philosophy is itself a philosophical question. There are, of course, areas that are clearly philosophical which have not been discussed as much as they should. Until fairly recently, one of these was the status and nature of logic itself. This was a key concern to the founders of modern logic, especially those that advocated intuitionism. But, partly as a result of Quine's insistence that first-order classical logic should be viewed as *the* logic, the philosophy *of* logic has become a very specialized topic, predominantly for logicians.

Inasmuch as philosophy seeks to construct valid arguments and a valid argument rests on the idea of the conclusions following from the premises, it seems essential for philosophers to say what they mean by 'following from.' Deciding on this issue has a great impact on one's choice of logic, be it classical or constructive. There are good arguments, for example, for reading 'implication' as *relevant* implication; in this way at least, we avoid the strange consequences of material implication (for example, we would not normally say that, for any propositions p and q, either $p \to q$ or $q \to p$; but this is a logical truth when '$\to$' is read as material implication).

Just as we do not have a fixed and universal notion of what 'following from,' 'implication' or 'entailment' mean, we do not have a fixed account of conditionals in natural language either. A truth-functional analysis of the indicative conditional 'if ... then ...' in terms of material implication does not seem right. Material implication is linked to our classical conception of consequence and proof by the deduction theorem: $p \to q$ is valid iff $p \models q$ iff $p \vdash q$. But if what we mean by 'if ... then ...' does not correspond to material implication, in what sense should we hold that our arguments, as we state them in English, are formalized by classical logic?

These issues should be thought of as core areas of analytic philosophy. I should mention that there has been plenty of work on these issues recently. Just to mention a few examples, both Graham Priest and Greg Restall discuss the philosophy of logic in a way that is undeniably relevant to mainstream philosophy. Priest discusses Dialethism, the view that there are true contradictions. In classical logic, the presence of a contradiction in a formal system implies triviality: all propositions whatsoever follow from the contradiction. But even if there really do exist true contradictions, there remain propositions that are not true and so a *paraconsistent* notion of consequence is required, that is, one that allows for certain contradictions without triviality. Restall offers the position of logical pluralism: the view that whilst there is not one true logic, we should not be relativists about logical consequence.

An issue that needs to be addressed in epistemology is, when we speak of an agent entertaining an attitude (such as knowledge, desire or belief), just what are we assuming about the agent? In particular, what are we assuming about the rationality or the reasoning abilities of the agent? It is in a sense irrational to form contradictory intentions: an agent that says she intends to open and close the door at one and the same time is surely in a very confused state! But this case is intuitively different from that of a mathematician who intends (and so attempts) to prove a mathematical hypothesis, which then turns out to be impossible. Similarly, most agents have inconsistent beliefs, yet we still believe ourselves to be rational, more or less.

The issue is, when we ascribe states of belief or desire to an agent, are we taking the agent to be an ideal reasoner, or an irrational thinker, or something in between? There is always a degree of idealization at play in epistemology, for example when I suggested above that an agent who knows that $p \wedge q$ also knows that p. That is, we assume this on behalf of the agent, just from the fact that we are assigning psychological attitudes, a precondition of which is that we treat the agent as (more or less) rational. But we need to be clear just what we mean by this and how far we should take the idealization. As I mentioned above, it certainly sounds strange to take the idealization to its extreme and say that every agent knows every valid sentence automatically, even if it has never explicitly considered that sentence before. A relevant question here is, just how hard is it for the agent to obtain a certain piece of knowledge, given what else it knows? This invites us to consider the complexity of knowledge acquisition and so links epistemology to complexity theory, which I discussed above. This will be an interesting area for formal epistemology in the coming years.

What are the most important open problems in philosophy and what are the prospects for progress?

In a sense, all philosophical problems are open and all are important; this is in part what makes them philosophical problems in the first place. What is important about philosophy—what makes it essential, rather than just an academic pursuit—is the thought that, through studying philosophy, we can understand our world and what it means to us more clearly. The age-old philosophical problems of truth, meaning and knowledge are unlikely to go away; we will not move into a phase of philosophy in which they are deemed unimportant or the wrong questions.

This is not to say that philosophy is isolated from the progress of science; development in the sciences has always inspired philosophical thought. Seventeenth Century science had its impact on John Locke's views on perception and the formulation of quantum physics has given new life to the debate on chance and determinism, for example. The development of mathematical logic in the late nineteenth and early twentieth century is perhaps the scientific development that has affected contemporary philosophy the most, for the rise of analytic philosophy is inseparable from the development of logic.

In the early twenty-first century, developments in cognitive science and neuroscience are sure to have an impact on philosophical thought. Explaining how we experience the world as we do is a task for scientists and philosophers alike; the one group is unlikely to arrive at a satisfactory answer without the other. Part of the philosopher's task here will be to reconcile the phenomenal aspect of experience with the developing scientific view of cognition. As to the extent that formal philosophy will play in this enterprise, we shall have to wait and see.

11

Edwin Mares

Associate Professor of Philosophy
Centre for Logic, Language, and Computation
Victoria University of Wellington, New Zealand

Why were you initially drawn to formal methods?

I love structure and patterns. I always enjoyed physics and mathematics at school and when I found logic and saw that there is a formal, structural, and mathematical way to describe reality in its most general aspects I was thrilled.

What example(s) from your work illustrates the role formal methods can play in philosophy?

Like Wittgenstein, I think that Russell's theory of descriptions is the greatest single work in formal philosophy. It showed how to deal with a problem – negative existentials – in a clear way. And it introduced us to a scope distinction that no one had previously known to exist. Regardless of whether one thinks that the theory of descriptions really solves the whole problem of apparent reference to non-entities, it does provide a solution to one aspect of that problem. And in so doing, it illustrates the possibility of there being formal solutions to other very difficult problems.

Formal methods can play two roles in philosophy. First, as in the case of Russell's theory of descriptions, logic can be used to solve or illuminate philosophical problems. For example, it has helped us to provide a compositional semantics for natural language, help us to understand scientific method (here the work of the strucuturalists is particularly instructive), and help understand the basic structure of reasoning (in both descriptive and normative senses). Second, logic has also become a subject of study for philosophy. The debate over the nature of belief reports is largely a (rather instructive) debate over the logic of belief reports. Similarly the debate about the nature of the conditional is a debate about logic and about how to formalize natural language conditionals. In providing a subject matter for philosophy, both logic and philosophy gain. Logicians have been forced to modify their theories (e.g. in producing ever more logics of conditionals) and philosophers consequently need to integrate these new theories into their own beliefs and change other views (about mind, language, ethics, and everything else) in accordance with them.

One nice example where philosophers have been forced to integrate a logical theory is the semantics of modal logic. Our best (and really only) available semantics for modal logic or counterfactuals is a possible world semantics. Given this, metaphysicians have had to take on board possible worlds. Now, this doesn't mean that every contemporary metaphysician believes that there are alternative possible worlds – there are fictionalists and instrumentalists – but every one worth her salt does have some way of understanding possible world semantics. The attempt to integrate possible worlds into the various metaphysical positions has been an extremely fruitful process for philosophy.

In terms of my own work, most of my recent philosophical work has been to provide a philosophical interpretation for my own favourite logic, the logic R of relevant implication discovered by Alonzo Church and developed by Alan Anderson and Nuel Belnap. My work that illustrates this attempt most clearly and completely is my book, *Relevant Logic: A Philosophical Interpretation* (Cambridge: Cambridge University Press, 2004). In this book, I try to integrate relevant logic into the mainstream of logical and metaphysical thought and also to bring into the mainstream some other theories that have been treated as rather marginal by philosophical community, in particular the theory of non-well-founded sets.

What is the proper role of philosophy in relation to other disciplines?

Philosophy and the sciences have had an often close, but often fractious relationship. Contemporary philosophy seems split in its attitude towards science along analytic/post-modernist lines. Back in the 1980s one often heard post-modernists complain about 'scientism' and we still see Latour and others attacking science. On the other hand, analytic philosophers often seem slavish in their attitude towards science. We tend to say that whatever the scientific community accepts is fine with us. (This includes contemporary anti-realists.) We tend not to be revisionists about science. More importantly, there is a tendency among contemporary philosophers of science to point out bad science only after it has been rejected by the scientific community. If our views on methodology are to have any real impact in the sciences, we probably should become more proactive and indicate what is bad science when we see it coming.

Philosophy of mathematics would seem to be quite different. Philosophers of mathematics are often revisionists—we have intuitionists, strict finitists, and the like, in addition to hard line Platonists who hold that classical mathematics is just fine the way it is. But there is more to this story. The original revisionists have usually been mathematicians, not people who primarily consider themselves to be philosophers. Of course we have revisionists like Dummett, who do self-identify as philosophers, but only after mathematicians such as Brouwer have already developed the revisionary mathematics that the philosophers adopt (and, in the case of Dummett, reinterpret).

What I am saying is that I think that philosophers should become bolder. Philosophy should be of some use to non-philosophers and unless we make ourselves heard, it won't be.

What do you consider the most neglected topics and/or contributions in late 20th century philosophy?

I think that philosophy of history is far too neglected. The debates in that field seem to date back to the thirties and not much progress seems to have been made since the 1960s. It is due for a rethink.

The philosophy of category theory has been developing too slowly. It is time to shift the attention of philosophers of mathematics away from sets to categories.

Although there is some recent interesting work in the field, pragmatics has received too little attention from philosophers of language (and logicians). Understanding how we understand conversation is crucial to our understanding of language, inference, and ourselves.

It is otherwise hard to think of anything very neglected. After the deluge of encyclopedias, handbooks, guides, and companions to every branch of philosophy in the past few years, it seems that every possible topic has been discussed recently.

What are the most important open problems in philosophy and what are the prospects for progress?

For logic, providing natural language with a semantics seems the most pressing problem. We have some powerful tools to do so: discourse representation theory, categorical grammars, and the like. But we have no widely accepted solutions to the main problems in the field (the structure of belief reports, the nature of anaphora, etc.). And no tie in with theories of pragmatics or a link with informal theories about how we reason have really been made.

In metaethics, the problem of moral objectivity. The idea that there might not be a set of objective moral standards is too horrible for many of us to contemplate. There is an objective right and wrong, damn it! But what are they and how can we tell what they are?

For philosophy more generally, a problem (though not an open problem in the usual sense) is where to go from here. We are at an odd juncture. There are no towering figures right now to set the agenda. The big figures of the late 20th Century are almost all dead, and the others are no longer producing ground-breaking work. Although there is a very large number of extremely good philosophers out there, no one seems to be rising to take the lead. In one way this is good: It is good for individual philosophers that we do not have an agenda set for us. But it isn't good for the discipline. Although there are fashions and fads in contemporary philosophy, no one seems to be working on a big project that has captured the imagination of the masses (in particular of students who might otherwise come into philosophy). We are a bit at drift at the moment.

The prospects for progress? I'd hate to predict.

12

Greg Restall

Professor of Philosophy
Department of Philosophy
University of Melbourne, Australia

Why were you initially drawn to formal methods?

I suppose the natural way to interpret this question is something like "why do formal methods rather than anything else in philosophy" but in my case I'd rather answer the related question "why, given that you're interested in formal methods, apply them in philosophy rather than elsewhere." I started off my academic life as an undergraduate student in mathematics, because I was good at mathematics and studying it more seemed like a good idea at the time.

I enjoyed mathematics a great deal. At the University of Queensland, where I was studying, there was a special cohort of "Honours" students right from the first year. You were taught more research-oriented and rigourous subjects than were provided for the "Pass" students. This meant that we had a small cohort of students, who knew each other pretty well, studied together and learned a lot. I could see myself making an academic career in mathematics. (I surely couldn't see myself doing anything other than an academic career. Being around the university was too much fun.)

However, there was a fly in the ointment. I was doing well in my studies, but I was losing the *feel* for a great deal of the mathematics I was doing. Applied mathematics went first, and analysis soon after. I could do the work, but I didn't *understand* it. I wrote assignments by matching patterns from what I had written in my lecture notes, or what was in the text with what we were asked. In exams, I just bashed away at the problem, sometimes when asked in an exam to prove that $A = B$, I'd work at A from the top of a page and keep manipulating it until I'd got stuck. Then I'd work backwards from B, hoping to meet at somewhere rather like where I'd got stuck. If I was honest, I'd write "I don't know how to get from here to there". If I was dishonest, I'd just leave the transition unexplained. Knowing what I know now about marking assignments, it doesn't suprise me that I did very well.

The areas where intuition and understanding lasted the longest (and which were the most *fun*) were topology, probability theory, combinatorics, set theory and logic. There were so few honours subjects I really wanted to do that in my last year I struck a deal with the mathematics department that I could do a reading course in logic with the newly arrived professor in the Philosophy Department. The professor was Graham Priest, and the reading course was my introduction to philosophical logic.

At the very same time as I was wondering how to continue with academic life. I was very involved in Christian student things: in the little group I was in, I ran study groups, I organised meetings, I wrote publicity material, and I did a bucketload of reading. In particular, while trying to figure out what I believed about things (about a lot of things), I read a lot of philosophy of religion and other philosophy written by Christians. I found the philosophy more interesting, more rigourous and more accessible than a great deal of the theology I had been reading. This piqued my interest in doing more philosophy for myself. I hadn't done much philosophy as an undergraduate (just two subjects), but I started trying to figure out how to do a major in Philosophy quickly, so that I could go on to postgraduate work in that field, rather than in mathematics.

It turned out that my work with Graham Priest went so well that I didn't need to do more undergraduate study in Philosophy to start postgraduate work (That semester course resulted in my first genuine academic publication [5]) I was offered a place in the Ph.D. program on the strength of my background in mathematics. I was free to pursue my interest in philosophy, and logic was the bridge. This meant that I could use the formal, mathematical skills that I had learned, on topics that interested me, and that I understood. The mathematics was simple and manageable, it was applied to interesting issues, and I got to hang around with philosophers, who are interesting people.

What example(s) from your work illustrates the role formal methods can play in philosophy?

I'll take an example from my recent work on proof theory and its application in philosophy [6, 8]. In the last few years I have been working on topics in proof theory and connections between the way we can conceive of the structure of proofs and concerns in the theory of meaning. The idea that the meaning of a word or a concept might be usefully explicated by giving an account of its inferential role is a common one — the work of Ned Block, Bob Brandom and Michael Dummett are three very different examples of ways to take this idea seriously. It is a truism that meaning has *some* sort of connection with use, and use in reasoning and inference is a very important part of any account of use.

It has seemed to me that if we are going to take inferential role as playing its part in a theory of meaning, then we had better use the best available tools for giving an account of proof. The theory of proofs should have something to teach philosophers who have interests in semantics. This is not a mainstream position — our vocabulary itself speaks against this, with the ready identification of model theory with 'semantics' and proof theory with 'syntax'. The work of intuitionists such as Dummett, Prawitz, Martin-Löf and Tennant is conspicuous in its isolation at providing a contrary opinion to the mainstream. This has led to the opinion that semantically anti-realist positions — those that take proof or inference as the starting point of semantic theory, rather than truth-conditions or representation — are naturally revisionary and intuitionist. For intuitionistic logic has a clear motivation in terms of proof and verification, and it has seemed to many that orthodox classical logic does not.

I think that this is a mistake. It seems to me that natural proof-theoretic accounts of classical logic (starting with Gentzen's sequent calculus, but also newer pieces of technology such as proof-nets [6, 9]) can have a central place in a theory of meaning that starts with inferential role and not with truth. We can think of the valid sequents (of the form $X \vdash Y$, where X and Y are sets of statements) as helping us 'keep score' in dialectical positions. The validity of the sequent $X \vdash Y$ tells us that a position in dialogue in which each statement in X is asserted and each statement in Y is denied is out of bounds according to the rules of 'the game.' In fact, the structural rules in the sequent calculus can be motivated in this way. Identity sequents $X, A \vdash A, Y$ tell us that asserting and denying A (in the same context) are out of bounds. The rule of weakening tells us that if asserting X and denying Y is out of bounds then adding an extra assertion or extra denial would not aid the matter. The cut rule tells us that if a position in which X is asserted and Y is denied is not out of bounds, then given a statement A, either the addition as an assertion, or its addition as a denial will also not be out of bounds. If asserting A is out of bounds in a context, it is implicitly denied in that context. Explicitly denying is no worse than implicitly denying.

Thinking of Gentzen's sequent calculus in this way gives an alternative understanding of classical logic. We think of the rules for connectives as 'definitions' governing assertions featuring the logical vocabulary. Proof-theoretical techniques such as the eliminability of the 'cut' rule tell us that these definitions are *conservative*. No matter what the rules of the game concerning our primitive vocabulary might be, we can add the classical logical connectives without disturbing the rules of assertion in that primitive vocabulary [1]. The logical vocabulary allows us to 'make explicit' what was merely 'implicit' before [2]. The interpretation of the rules of the quantifiers is particularly enlightening. It allows us to sidestep the debate between 'substitutional' and 'objectual' accounts of quantification [4].

In my recent work I have tried to flesh out this picture, and to show how we can expand this story to take account of appropriate conditions for use for modal connectives such as possibility and necessity. The key idea is that in modal discourse we not only assert and deny, but we make assertions and denials in different dialectical contexts, and an assertion of a necessity claim in one context can impinge on claims in other dialectical contexts [6]. This means that we can give a semantics of modal vocabulary that motivates a well-known modal logic (in the first instance, the simple modal logic **S5**, but the extension to other logics is not difficult) in which possible worlds are not the starting point of semantic explanation. Modal vocabulary needs not be conceived of as a way of describing possible worlds. It can be understood as a governing discourse in which we not only assert and deny to express our own commitments, but also to articulate the connections between our concepts. The structures of dialectical positions need not merely contain assertions and denials, but these may be partitioned into different 'zones' according to the structure of the different suppositions and shifts of context in that discourse.

12. Greg Restall

What is the proper role of philosophy in relation to other disciplines?

I find it very hard to isolate one single role for philosophy to play in relation to other academic disciplines. Philosophy and the other disciplines are complicated things and interaction between them should occur in many different ways. I will focus on one aspect of philosophy's relationship to other disciplines that I think is worth highlighting, and which does not receive as much attention as it should.

Frege's revolutionary account of quantification – which has been so important in so many areas of philosophy – was motivated by trying to understand the structure and content of mathematical reasoning. In just this way, other philosophical tools and techniques can be informed by motivations outside philosophy. Contemporary predicate logic with quantifiers and variables is such an advance over Aristotelian logic because it provides a natural and perspicuous way to understand reasoning in mathematics. The Bolzano-Weierstrass ϵ–δ account of continuity that revolutionised calculus did not fit well with an Aristotelian understanding of logical validity. On an Aristotelian view we cannot straightforwardly *state* the condition for the continuity of a function f at a point x: $(\forall \epsilon > 0)(\exists \delta > 0)(\text{if } |x' - x| < \epsilon \text{ then } |f(x') - f(x)| < \delta)$, let alone give an account that explains why the mathematicians' reasoning is actually correct. New work in logic and philosophy arose out of attempting this task of understanding and articulating mathematical reasoning. (This story is clearly told in Albert Coffa's *The Semantic Tradition* [3].)

This feature of philosophical research is a general one: Some of the best and richest work in philosophy is done in trying to understand X, where X is some discipline that is not necessarily itself obviously 'philosophical.' The job of a philosopher and a logician is not only (and not even *primarily*) to be an intellectual hygienist who cleans up the messy reasoning of our colleagues in other disciplines. We perform a much more useful function when we learn from the specialist X-theorists (whatever field X might be) who develop new ways of doing things in their own fields. Philosophers can be one avenue of communication between disciplines, as we attempt to incorporate the findings of different fields into a general, coherent picture of the world. In logic, a crucial X for the last 200 years has been mathematics, but it is clear that now computer science is also playing a role. New work in logic in computer science is finding its way into philosophical logic, and expanding the field yet more [7].

What do you consider the most neglected topics and/or contributions in late 20th century philosophy?

I think that something we philosophers do not expect so much is that the revolution in logic and our understanding of the form and structure of what we can say is a revolution that is ongoing. The 19th and 20th Century overthrow of the Aristotelian conception of the fundamental logical form of judgement has yet to work its way through our conceptual scheme. Many philosophers to this day conceive of every judgement as a predication of a property to an object, despite our best understanding of logic showing us that many things we say cannot be viewed in this way. Other views (think of Quine, as one influential example) take it that anything that can be said can be said in the language of first-order classical predicate logic. I think that contemporary work in logic will continue to a kind of revolutionary impact on our conception of the significance of our own language and concepts. As we find more and more interesting, appropriate and useful ways of conceiving of the structure and semantics of our language this will have significant consequences throughout philosophy. This kind of constructive work in logic can play its role in the perennial philosophical trio of understanding the relationship between mind, world and language (or, if you like, between thought, action and talk).

For example, current debates over the significance of modal logic are not merely sterile ontological questions of metaphysics. It is not so interesting to be concerned merely over whether or not you should be happy with the ontological extravagance of possible worlds. It seems to me that the much more interesting question concerning modal vocabulary concerns how we wire up the connection between the modal concepts and our world. How do modal concepts work? What are we talking *about* when we make judgements of possibility and necessity? Just what can we *say* with our modal ideology? These questions are not merely a matter of semantics in the thin sense of providing a catalogue of the way that we use the terminology. It is the much more interesting task of giving an account of the proper functioning of an important segment of our conceptual scheme. The best work in philosophical logic plays its own role, contributing to these questions, and telling a central part of the story of how mind, world and language relate to one another.

What are the most important open problems in philosophy and what are the prospects for progress?

New ways of conceiving the relationship between belief, speech-acts and propositions will provide a rich way of understanding our place in the world and our thought and talk about that world. The question of how we ought to understand semantics is not so much an open 'problem,' but a wide open field of debate in which there is a great deal of room for the development of options and rival programs. These options impinge on many different issue in philosophy. I will give two examples of how this debate plays out.

EXAMPLE 1: META-ETHICS. Central questions in moral philosophy involve crucial semantic issues. Different options in semantics play an important role in debates in moral philosophy — can we give an *expressivist* account of the siginficance and semantics of moral terminology? For example, Simon Blackburn's moral 'quasi-realism' hinges on a non truth-conditional account of the meaning of moral vocabulary. Can this account succeed? Any account of the significance of our moral vocabulary will take a position on these core semantic issues. Logic and semantics here act not so much as arbiter between different positions, but a field of investigation providing options for the development of particular projects in meta-ethics.

EXAMPLE 2: PHILOSOPHY OF MIND. Semantic issues play also their part in questions in the philosophy of mind. Our understanding of mental concepts and the relationship between mental states and physical states turns on questions of the understanding of modality and analyticity. The application of so-called 'two-dimensional modal logic' in articulating these issues shows that the possible positions we can take on the mind-body problem hinge on views of modal semantics.

In these kinds of philosophical debates, the role of logic is not merely one of being a neutral arbiter between competing positions. The role is much more important than this, and playing the part is much more interesting and engaging. The fact that logic plays an expressive role means that we logicians can help provide new ways of conceiving the significance of what we can say about the world and our place in it.

What is the scope for *progress* on these issues? It seems to me that we will have made progress in philosophical questions if we have a broad and diverse community of people engaging in the distinctive mix of critical and creative work that is philosophical logic, engaged with issues in philosophy and other disciplines in the academy. The world of the late 20th Century has been one of increasing academic specialisation and isolation between experts in distinctive fields with their own problems and traditions, tools and techniques. I hope that in the 21st Century, the globalisation of communication will foster new and exciting bridges of collaboration between philosophical logicians and others working within philosophy and those working outside it, from different traditions and backgrounds. In this way our understanding of the world and our place in it stands to be expanded and enriched, challenged and renewed. I hope that it will be to the benefit of us all. *That would be progress.*

[1] Nuel D. Belnap. Tonk, plonk and plink. *Analysis*, 22: 130–134, 1962.

[2] Robert B. Brandom. *Making It Explicit*. Harvard University Press, 1994.

[3] J. Alberto Coffa. *The Semantic Tradition from Kant to Carnap*. Cambridge University Press, 1993. Edited by LindaWessels.

[4] Mark Lance. Quantification, substitution, and conceptual content. *Noûs*, 30(4): 481–507, 1996.

[5] Greg Restall. A note on naïve set theory in LP. *Notre Dame Journal of Formal Logic*, 33: 422–432, 1992.

[6] Greg Restall. Proofnets for s5: sequents and circuits for modal logic. To appear in the *Proceedings of the 2006 Logic Colloquium*, 200+.

[7] Greg Restall. *An Introduction to Substructural Logics*. Routledge, 2000.

[8] Greg Restall. Multiple conclusions. In Petr Hájek, Luis ValdésVillanueva, and Dag Westerståhl, editors, *Logic, Methodology and Philosophy of Science: Proceedings of the Twelfth International Congress*, pages 189–205. KCL Publications, 2005.

[9] Edmund Robinson. Proof nets for classical logic. *Journal of Logic and Computation*, 13(5): 777–797, 2003.

Offprints of papers are available at http://consequently.org/writing

13
John F. Sowa

Croton-on-Hudson, NY, USA

Why were you initially drawn to formal methods?

My academic degrees are in mathematics and computer science, but I have always had a strong interest in linguistics and philosophy. The interest in linguistics developed from my bilingual childhood, when my maternal grandmother, who lived with us, spoke only Polish at home. My interest in mathematics began with 10th grade geometry, when we were introduced to methods of theorem proving. I had been bored with the exercises in arithmetic and algebra, but I enjoyed the proofs in geometry. In the 11th grade, I bought the four-volume *World of Mathematics*, and I was especially intrigued by the articles on the foundations of mathematics. My father wanted me to study engineering, but I chose to major in mathematics at MIT, but with additional courses in physics, philosophy, and languages.

After graduating from MIT, I worked at IBM on a variety of research and development projects, primarily on programming languages, software systems, and artificial intelligence. To satisfy IBM management, I had to demonstrate that my work had commercial relevance. By pursuing computational linguistics, I was able to combine my interests in linguistics, philosophy, and mathematics in a form that promised to have important applications.

In the early 1970s, I was impressed by the work of Richard Montague, but I doubted that his cumbersome notation could characterize the cognitive processes of an infant who was learning language. My own bilingualism convinced me that language-independent concepts are central to semantics and that Chomsky's syntactic structures are reflections of more fundamental conceptual structures. My research on conceptual graphs was stimulated by the semantic networks of artificial intelligence (Sowa 1992), the dependency graphs by Tesnière (1959), and the existential graphs by Peirce (1909). What is most striking about Peirce's graphs are the elegant rules of inference, which can perform all operations of deduction by inserting, erasing, and copying graphs. Besides being precise, elegant, and powerful, those rules are simple enough to be cognitively realistic. After beginning my study of Peirce's philosophy with his graphs, I came to agree with him that they are central to all areas of semiotics, which, as Peirce claimed, encompasses all aspects of language, logic, knowledge, and reasoning.

What example(s) from your work illustrates the role formal methods can play in philosophy?

The most common formal methods are based on the algebraic notation for logic that Peirce introduced in 1880 and 1885. Yet a dozen years later, Peirce developed his existential graphs, which he believed were a more perspicuous representation for logic. Since both notations are equivalent in expressive power, most logicians saw no reason to prefer graphs to their familiar algebraic formulas. Yet the graph notation clarifies the logical structure and supports simpler and more efficient computational methods.

To illustrate the differences, consider the verb *give*, which is often represented by a triadic relation, as in the following formula for the sentence *Sue gives a child a book*:

$$(\exists x)(\exists y)(\text{Person}(\text{Sue}) \land \text{Child}(x) \land \text{Book}(y) \land \text{Gives}(\text{Sue},x,y)). \tag{13.1}$$

Davidson (1967) recommended an alternative, usually called *event semantics*, in which the act of giving is treated as an entity in the domain of discourse, which may be linked to the participants by dyadic relations:

$$(\exists x)(\exists y)(\exists z)(\text{Person}(\text{Sue}) \land \text{Child}(x) \land \text{Book}(y) \land \text{Give}(z) \land \text{Agnt}(z,\text{Sue}) \land \text{Rcpt}(z,x) \land \text{Thme}(z,y)). \tag{13.2}$$

In formula (2), the variable z represents an event of giving, which is linked to the participants by dyadic relations that represent the *case relations* or *thematic roles* of linguistics: Sue is the agent (**Agnt**) of giving, the child is the recipient (**Rcpt**), and the book is the theme (**Thme**).

Although the option of letting quantifiers range over events is widely used in both theoretical and computational linguistics,

Strawson (1992) criticized it as unrealistic and unnecessary: "What could be more simple and straightforward than the idea of a construction whereby we may tack on to the verbs of happening or action in such sentences a phrase which answers these when? and where? questions" (p. 104). In fact, that is exactly what a graph logic does: it represents concepts and relations in a systematic way that allows any number of links to be "tacked on" for any relations, properties, or modifiers that may be expressed in a sentence. Figure (13.1) shows two conceptual graphs that are logically equivalent to formulas (1) and (2).

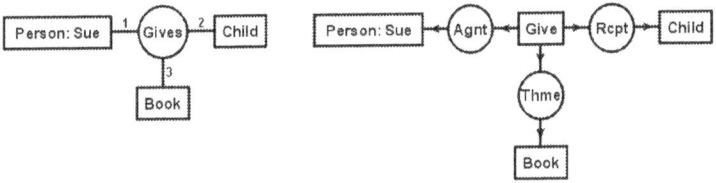

FIGURE 13.1. Two conceptual graphs for *Sue gives a child a book*

In the CG on the left of Figure (13.1), the circle represents an instance of the triadic relation Gives, which relates Sue to the child and the book. Each box represents a concept node with a *type label*, such as Person, and an optional name, such as Sue. As in Peirce's existential graphs, the default quantifier is the existential. Therefore, the CG on the left would be mapped to formula (1). The CG on the right, which would be mapped to formula (2), represents the verb *gives* with the concept type Give, and the three circles represent the dyadic relations in formula (2). The arrow pointing toward a relation represents the first argument, and the arrow pointing away represents the second argument; for relations with more than two arguments, the links are numbered. Peirce coined the term *hypostatic abstraction* for the method of replacing a relation by a quantified node in a graph, and he generalized it to properties and relations represented by any part of speech in natural languages.

As Figure (13.1) illustrates, the graph notation avoids the complexity that Strawson considered "unnecessary and unrealistic" while representing exactly the same logical information as the formula. One reason why the graphs are simpler than the formulas is that each entity is represented by a single node to which all associated relations are attached. The child, for example, is represented by a single node [Child] in either of the two graphs, but it is represented by three occurrences of the variable x in formula (1) and four occurrences of x in formula (2). Figure (13.2), which represents the sentence *At 2 pm, Sue graciously gave the poor child a new book*, shows how more relations can be linked to various concept nodes.

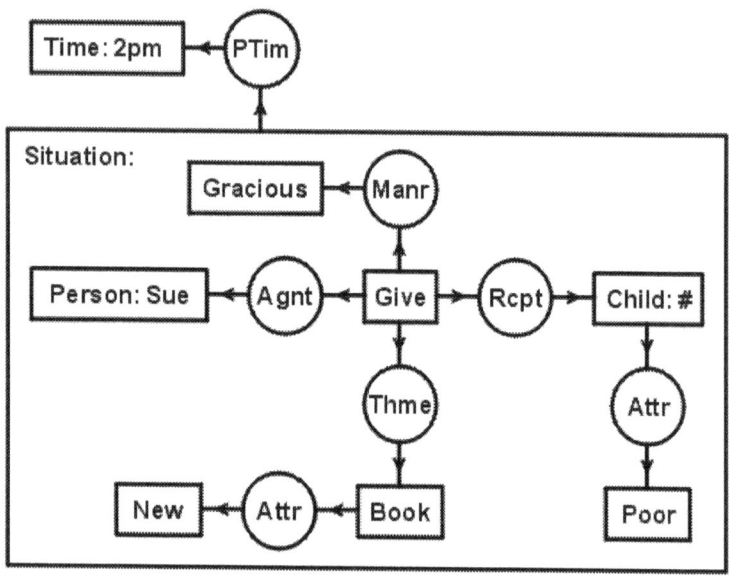

FIGURE 13.2. CG for *At 2 pm, Sue graciously gave the poor child a new book*

Nested conceptual graphs, as in Figure (13.2), can represent propositions at different metalevels, modalities, or tenses (Sowa 2003). The large box represents a concept of type Situation, which occurs at the point in time (PTim) 2 pm. That situation is described by a nested CG, which has some additional modifiers for the manner relation (Manr), which links [Give] to an instance of graciousness, and for the attribute relations (Attr), which link the book to an instance of newness and the child to an instance of poverty. These concepts are hypostatic abstractions of properties, to which relations can be attached to modify the degree of newness or to compare one person's poverty to another's. More than 70 years before Davidson, Peirce discussed such abstractions and used quantified variables to refer to them. The concept [Child: #] uses the symbol # to mark the *indexical* expressed by the definite article *the*. Since predicate calculus does not represent indexicals, the symbol # must be resolved to a name or variable that designates a specific individual in the context before the CG can be translated to other notations for logic. If some other statement had identified the child as Bob, then the referent of the concept would be resolved to [Child: Bob], and the CG could be translated to formula (3):

$(\exists s)(\text{Situation}(s) \land \text{Time}(2\text{pm}) \land \text{Ptim}(s, 2\text{pm}) \land \text{dscr}(s,$
$(\exists y)(\exists z)(\exists u)(\exists v)(\exists w)(\text{Person}(\text{Sue}) \land \text{Child}(\text{Bob}) \land$
$\text{Book}(y) \land \text{Give}(z) \land \text{Gracious}(u) \land \text{Poor}(v) \land \text{New}(w) \land$
$\text{Manr}(z, u) \land \text{Attr}(\text{Bob}, v) \land \text{Attr}(y, w) \land \text{Agnt}(z, \text{Sue}) \land$
$\text{Rcpt}(z, \text{Bob}) \land \text{Thme}(z, y))))$.

(13.3)

These techniques, which Peirce invented over a century ago, have enabled conceptual graphs to represent many other proposed formalisms, including the equivalent of *situation semantics* (Barwise & Perry 1983) and *discourse representation structures* (Kamp & Reyle 1993). They can support all the modalities and intensional verbs of Kripke and Montague, but with a simpler formal structure (Sowa 2003).

What is the proper role of philosophy in relation to other disciplines?

I believe that philosophy should play its traditional role: to provide a synoptic view that relates, critiques, and integrates all areas of human thought. That role is orthogonal to the goal of making philosophy more scientific, which is not bad in itself, but which has had the side effect of making philosophy as specialized as any field of science. As a result, the broader philosophical issues have been ignored or left to politicians and preachers. Philosophy departments are losing enrollments, and the philosophy shelves at bookstores are squeezed into a corner behind the books on astrology, witchcraft, and religious fundamentalism of every stripe.

I have the greatest admiration for Peirce and Whitehead, two logicians who did not consider any traditional area of philosophy to be outside their scope. In fact, Peirce's *first rule of reason* implies that no question is illegitimate:

> Upon this first, and in one sense this sole, rule of reason, that in order to learn you must desire to learn, and

in so desiring not be satisfied with what you already incline to think, there follows one corollary which itself deserves to be inscribed upon every wall of the city of philosophy: Do not block the way of inquiry. (CP 1.135)

Although Peirce was highly critical of most of the writings on metaphysics, he was even harsher on the positivists, such as Ernst Mach, who tried to banish metaphysics:

> Find a scientific man who proposes to get along without any metaphysics – not by any means every man who holds the ordinary reasonings of metaphysicians in scorn – and you have found one whose doctrines are thoroughly vitiated by the crude and uncriticized metaphysics with which they are packed. We must philosophize, said the great naturalist Aristotle — if only to avoid philosophizing. Every man of us has a metaphysics, and has to have one; and it will influence his life greatly. Far better, then, that that metaphysics should be criticized and not be allowed to run loose. (CP 1.129)

As an example of the vitiating effect of his crude metaphysics, Mach fought a long, desperate battle against the assumption of unobservable atoms and prevented his fellow Viennese, Ludwig Boltzmann, from receiving proper recognition for his brilliant theory of statistical mechanics (Lindley 2001). Einstein was even more blunt: "Mach was a good experimental physicist but a miserable philosopher"; he made "a catalog not a system" (quoted by Lindley, p. 219).

Whitehead (1929) constructed one of the largest and most ambitious metaphysical systems of the 20th century, but Russell, Carnap, and other logical positivists wrote polemics against metaphysics. To eliminate metaphysical assumptions, Russell (1924) formulated what he called "the supreme axiom in scientific philosophising": "Whenever possible, substitute constructions out of known entities for inferences to unknown entities" (p. 363). Einstein (1944) criticized Russell's "fear of metaphysics" (Angst vor der Metaphysik) as a "malady (Krankheit) of contemporary empiricist philosophy." Contrary to Russell, Einstein maintained that "the concepts which arise in our thought and in our linguistic expressions are all – logically considered – free creations of thought which cannot be inductively derived from sense experiences"; he believed that was just as true "for everyday thinking as for the more consciously and systematically developed thought in the sciences."

Einstein rescued physics from the sterility of the positivists' prohibition against unobservable entities, but many psychologists and linguists did not have the courage to resist. The behaviorists were the most enthusiastic in purging their theories of all traces of unobservable mental notions; they even dropped the name *psychology* because it suggested an unobservable *psyche*. Although the behaviorists developed useful experimental and statistical techniques, they set back the theoretical developments by at least a half century. To see the effect, compare the 1890 *Principles of Psychology* by William James to the writings on cognitive psychology in the 1960s. In the range of topics and methodology, there is an unbroken continuity, not a 70-year gap.

In linguistics, the late 19th century was an active period of semantic exploration, which culminated in Peirce's semiotics, Saussure's semiology, and the lexicography of Roget's *Thesaurus*, the *Oxford English Dictionary*, and the *Century Dictionary*. In the first version of his textbook on linguistics, Bloomfield (1914) presented an approach to semantics based on Wundt's psychology. In the 1920s, however, Bloomfield was seduced by the behaviorists, and the second version of his textbook (Bloomfield 1933) avoided semantics. Even Chomsky (1957), who was highly critical of the behaviorists, honored their restrictions by developing his theories of syntax independent of semantics and lexicography. Katz and Fodor (1963) reintroduced a tiny amount of semantics through a negative formula: "Language description minus grammar is semantics." The great linguist Roman Jakobson, who had studied under an older tradition, countered with the slogan "Syntax without semantics is meaningless."

These examples from physics, psychology, and linguistics illustrate the importance of philosophy for the sciences. A philosophy that does not "block the way of inquiry" can enrich, clarify, and extend the development of scientific ideas. But a philosophy that imposes arbitrary restrictions can distract and stifle research for many decades.

What do you consider the most neglected topics and/or contributions in late 20th century philosophy?

I believe the major weaknesses of 20th century analytic philosophy could be characterized by Whitehead's remark as he introduced Russell for the William James lectures at Harvard: "I am pleased to introduce my good friend Bertrand Russell. Bertie thinks that I am muddle-headed, but then, I think that he is simple-minded"(Lucas 1989, p. 111). That remark is consistent with a statement attributed to Russell: "I'd rather be narrow minded than vague and woolly" (Kuntz 1984, p. 50).

The narrow focus began with Frege (1879), who set out "to break the domination of the word over the human spirit by laying bare the misconceptions that through the use of language often almost unavoidably arise concerning the relations between concepts." His strength lay in the clarity of his distinctions, which Frege (1884) summarized in three fundamental principles:

1. "always to separate sharply the psychological from the logical, the subjective from the objective;"

2. "never to ask for the meaning of a word in isolation, but only in the context of a proposition;"

3. "never to lose sight of the distinction between concept and object."

These distinctions may sound good in isolation, but in practice the borderlines are not clear. Instead of trying to understand the reasons for the lack of clarity, Frege imposed arbitrary restrictions:

> In compliance with the first principle, I have used the word "idea" always in the psychological sense, and have distinguished ideas from concepts and from objects. If the second principle is not observed, one is almost forced to take as the meanings of words mental pictures or acts of the individual mind, and so to offend against the first principle as well.

With this interpretation, Frege made it impossible to formalize metalanguage as language about language because there are no physical objects that can serve as the referents of metalevel terms. In the *Tractatus*, Wittgenstein (1921) observed Frege's restrictions and defined meaningful language in terms of references to physical objects and their relationships. Everything else, including his own analysis of language, had no legitimate reference: "My propositions are elucidatory in this way: he who understands me finally recognizes them as senseless" (6.54). In his later philosophy, Wittgenstein ignored that prohibition and criticized the "grave mistakes" in his first book.

In his book *Beyond Analytic Philosophy*, Hao Wang quoted a personal letter from C. I. Lewis about the state of philosophy in 1960:

> It is so easy... to get impressive 'results' by replacing the vaguer concepts which convey real meaning by virtue of common usage by pseudo precise concepts which are manipulable by 'exact' methods — the trouble being that nobody any longer knows whether anything actual or of practical import is being discussed. (p. 116)

Although precision is important for science, a precision that ignores the facts is an antiscientific, *a priori* obstacle to inquiry.

What are the most important open problems in philosophy and what are the prospects for progress?

The most important problems are the "vague and woolly" ones that the logical positivists tried to avoid. Wang (1986) observed that Carnap, in particular, was "willing to exclude an exceptionally large range of things on the grounds that they are 'not clear,' or sometimes that 'everything he says is poetry.'" But the logicians Peirce and Whitehead and the poet Robert Frost recognized that clarity is often an oversimplification. Whitehead (1937) aptly characterized the problem:

> Human knowledge is a process of approximation. In the focus of experience, there is comparative clarity. But the discrimination of this clarity leads into the penumbral background. There are always questions left over. The problem is to discriminate exactly what we know vaguely.

And Frost (1963) suggested the solution:

> I've often said that every poem solves something for me in life. I go so far as to say that every poem is a

momentary stay against the confusion of the world....
We rise out of disorder into order. And the poems I
make are little bits of order.

Contrary to Carnap, poetry and logic are not at opposite extremes. They are complementary approaches to closely related problems: developing patterns of symbols that capture important aspects of life in a memorable form.

Unlike Frege, Russell, and Carnap, Peirce did not avoid the challenge of characterizing the language people actually use by escaping to a purified realm of formal logic and ontology. He had been an associate editor of the *Century Dictionary*, for which he wrote, revised, or edited over 16,000 definitions. The combined influence of logic and lexicography is apparent in a letter he wrote to B.E. Smith, the editor of that dictionary:

> The task of classifying all the words of language, or what's the same thing, all the ideas that seek expression, is the most stupendous of logical tasks. Anybody but the most accomplished logician must break down in it utterly; and even for the strongest man, it is the severest possible tax on the logical equipment and faculty.

Since they were creating an unabridged dictionary, Peirce and his colleagues were forced to define every word that occurred in their corpus of citations. They dealt with language as it is, not as a logician might wish it to be. That is the first requirement for any scientific approach to language.

References

Barwise, Jon, & John Perry (1983) *Situations and Attitudes*, MIT Press, Cambridge, MA.

Bloomfield, Leonard (1914) *An Introduction to Language*, reprinted by J. Benjamins, Amsterdam, 1983.

Bloomfield, Leonard (1933) *Language*, Holt, Rinehart, & Winston, New York.

Chomsky, Noam (1957) *Syntactic Structures*, Mouton, The Hague.

Davidson, Donald (1967) "The logical form of action sentences," reprinted in D. Davidson (1980) *Essays on Actions and Events*, Clarendon Press, Oxford, pp. 105-148.

Einstein, Albert (1944) "Remarks on Bertrand Russell's Theory of Knowledge", in P. A. Schilpp, ed., *The Philosophy of Bertrand Russell*, Library of Living Philosophers.

Frege, Gottlob (1879) *Begriffsschrift*, English translation in J. van Heijenoort, ed. (1967) *From Frege to Gödel*, Harvard University Press, Cambridge, MA, pp. 1-82.

Frege, Gottlob (1884) *Die Grundlagen der Arithmetik*, tr. by J. L. Austin as *The Foundations of Arithmetic*, Blackwell, Oxford, 1953.

Frost, Robert (1963) *A Lover's Quarrel with the World* (film), WGBH Educational Foundation, Boston.

James, William (1890) *The Principles of Psychology*, Two volumes, Dover Publications, New York.

Kamp, Hans, & Uwe Reyle (1993) *From Discourse to Logic*, Kluwer, Dordrecht.

Katz, Jerrold J., & Jerry A. Fodor (1963) "The structure of a semantic theory," *Language* **39**, 170–210.

Kuntz, Paul Grimley (1984) *Alfred North Whitehead*, Twayne Publishers, Boston.

Lindley, David (2001) *Boltzmann's Atom: The Great Debate that Launched a Revolution in Physics*, Free Press, New York.

Lucas, George R., Jr. (1989) *The Rehabilitation of Whitehead*, State University of New York Press, Albany.

Peirce, Charles Sanders (1880) "On the algebra of logic," *American Journal of Mathematics* **3**, 15-57. Reprinted in W 4:163–209.

Peirce, Charles Sanders (1885) "On the algebra of logic," *American Journal of Mathematics* **7**, 180-202. Reprinted in W 5:162–190.

Peirce, Charles Sanders (1909) Manuscript 514, with commentary by J. F. Sowa, http://www.jfsowa.com/peirce/ms514.htm.

Peirce, Charles Sanders (CP) *Collected Papers of C. S. Peirce*, ed. by C. Hartshorne, P. Weiss, & A. Burks, 8 vols., Harvard University Press, Cambridge, MA, 1931-1958.

Peirce, Charles Sanders (W) *Writings of Charles S. Peirce*, vols. 1–6, Indiana University Press, Bloomington, 1982–1993.

Russell, Bertrand (1924) "Logical Atomism," in J. H. Muirhead, ed., *Contemporary British Philosophy*, London.

Sowa, John F. (1992) "Semantic networks," *Encyclopedia of Artificial Intelligence*, edited by S. C. Shapiro, Wiley, New York. Revised and extended version at http://www.jfsowa.com/pubs/semnet.htm.

Sowa, John F. (2003) "Laws, facts, and contexts: Foundations for multimodal reasoning," in *Knowledge Contributors*, edited by V. F. Hendricks, K. F. Jørgensen, and S. A. Pedersen, Kluwer Academic Publishers, Dordrecht, pp. 145–184.

Sowa, John F., & Arun K. Majumdar (2003) "Analogical reasoning," in A. de Moor, W. Lex, & B. Ganter, eds., *Conceptual Structures for Knowledge Creation and Communication*, LNAI 2746, Springer-Verlag, Berlin, pp. 16–36.

Strawson, Peter F. (1992) *Analysis and Metaphysics: An Introduction to Philosophy*, Oxford University Press, Oxford.

Tesnière, Lucien (1959) *Éléments de Syntaxe structurale*, 2nd edition, Librairie C. Klincksieck, Paris, 1965.

Wang, Hao (1986) *Beyond Analytic Philosophy: Doing Justice to What We Know*, MIT Press, Cambridge, MA.

Whitehead, Alfred North (1929) *Process and Reality: An Essay in Cosmology*, corrected edition edited by D. R. Griffin & D. W. Sherburne, Free Press, New York, 1978.

Whitehead, Alfred North (1937) "Analysis of Meaning," *Philosophical Review*, reprinted in A. N. Whitehead, *Essays in Science and Philosophy*, Philosophical Library, New York, pp. 122–131.

Wittgenstein, Ludwig (1921) *Tractatus Logico-Philosophicus*, Routledge & Kegan Paul, London.

14

Alasdair Urquhart

Professor of Philosophy
University of Toronto, Canada

Why were you initially drawn to formal methods?

As an undergraduate, I had vaguely mystical inclinations, and was attracted by the idea of non-rational insights in which the world would appear in some totally different light. Hegel's writings seemed to hint at a philosophy that encompassed such a realm of the super-rational. Bertrand Russell's *Introduction to Mathematical Philosophy* brought me down to earth with a bump. Russell's clear, hard-hitting prose attracted me immediately, as also the idea that formal mathematical work could lead to the solution of ancient philosophical problems.

Around the same time, I learned of Gödel's incompleteness results (I think through Nagel and Newman) and I resolved to learn enough logic to get a solid understanding of them. The latter half of my undergraduate career at Edinburgh University was devoted mostly to teaching myself logic, partly through *Principia Mathematica*, but also through close study of Martin Davis's wonderful anthology *The Undecidable*.

What example(s) from your work illustrates the role formal methods can play in philosophy?

The work of Gödel, Turing and others shows how simple conceptual analysis can lead to absolutely decisive results in the area of the foundations of mathematics. The power of logical and axiomatic analysis is extraordinary, and I see no reason why it should not be applied in further areas.

What is the proper role of philosophy in relation to other disciplines?

Philosophy as currently practiced in academic departments is more and more ingrown and scholastic in character. If philosophers are to have serious impact on other disciplines, they have to take the trouble to learn what is going on in these other disciplines. At the same time, it should be said that if philosophical logicians continue to work along lines that seem interesting to them, then their research may prove useful in other areas. This can be seen in the dramatic expansion of modal logic, temporal logic and epistemic logic in computer science, artificial intelligence and formal linguistics. I consider this very welcome development as one of the great success stories of *philosophical* logic over the last few decades.

What do you consider the most neglected topics and/or contributions in late 20th century philosophy?

Philosophers might well pay more attention to what is going on in areas like computer science, where new ideas of proof (for example) have emerged, and the idea of looking at epistemic agents with limited cognizing powers is basic. Philosophers working in epistemology have largely ignored this very interesting stream of work.

What are the most important open problems in philosophy and what are the prospects for progress?

I don't know enough of areas outside logic and the foundations of mathematics to make any sensible comment. In logic, I believe that the $P = ?NP$ problem is absolutely fundamental, and the most important and challenging question in logic. Whether you count this as a question in philosophy is a matter of taste, but it is worth recalling that Kurt Gödel already pointed out in a letter to John von Neumann in 1956 that a feasible solution to this problem would have extraordinarily strong consequences, such as the fact that mathematical discovery would be mechanisable in principle.

15
Heinrich Wansing

Professor of Philosophy of Science and Logic
Dresden University of Technology, Institute of Philosophy
Dresden, Germany

Ex formulis cognitio

Why were you initially drawn to formal methods?

Unsystematic reasons. When I took up my studies of philosophy and German language at the University of Düsseldorf in 1983, I was very quickly drawn to appreciating formal methods for several reasons. Some of my professors basically taught just empty rhetoric or historical facts (or both). I noticed, however, that there was also a small number of more interesting and remarkable scholars around, and it turned out that they were working in analytical philosophy and formal linguistics. Among them were Hartmut Brands, Axel Bühler, Gabriel Falkenberg, and Michael Sukale. When I changed to the Free University of Berlin in 1985, I was already firmly convinced that formal methods are indispensable in philosophy. In Berlin I studied philosophy with David Pearce, my later PhD thesis supervisor, and I attended lectures by Wolfgang Rautenberg at the Mathematics Department. David supported and influenced me in several ways. My first scientific paper was a paper co-authored with him, and we presented it at the 1988 Finnish-Soviet Logic Symposium. The symposium started in Helsinki, where there was a reception at Georg Henrik von Wright's place, and then the conference moved to Tampere. This was a very exciting meeting, both scientifically and because Perestroika was a topic in the background. David was in touch with many leading experts in logic and philosophy of science, and I remember that he brought several logicians and philosophers to Berlin for guest lectures and short visits, including, for example, Dov Gabbay, Peter Gärdenfors, David Makinson, Per Martin-Löf, and Ryszard Wójcicki. Moreover, David encouraged me to write to Johan van Benthem and to plan a research stay in Amsterdam after finishing my master's thesis in 1988, and I was very happy to be able to realize this stay with a grant from the German National Academic Foundation. In Amsterdam I met many excellent logicians and made acquaintance with quite a few other PhD students, including Patrick Blackburn, Wiebe van der Hoek, Maarten de Rijke, Yao-Hua Tan, Elias Thijsse, and Yde Venema, and several others. Later I was much influenced by Nuel Belnap and his work on the proof theory of non-classical logics and the modal logic of agency. Thus, I was partly drawn to formal methods, because I met some enthusiastic, inspiring, and excellent scientists who happened to use formal methods.

Systematic reasons. In addition to these historical and personal reasons, there are, of course, also systematic reasons that helped me to appreciate formal methods and to recognize their great importance and significance in philosophy. Theory formation in philosophy is sometimes in a poor state. It happens that a central notion is explicated in terms of other concepts that are as much in need of explanation as the notion of central concern. New terminology is introduced carelessly and a bewildering plenitude of concepts and neologisms sometimes makes it difficult to understand what is going on in certain areas and which insights have been obtained.

I would like to explain the systematic reasons why I came to appreciate formal methods in philosophy by means of two examples that do not, however, fit into the historical context of explaining why I was "initially" (and continuously) drawn to formal methods.

(i) In his quite recent monograph *Der mentale Zugang zur Welt* (Klostermann, Frankfurt/Main, 2003), Marcus Willaschek distinguishes between at least 512 versions of realism and anti-realism (with respect to everyday objects). This is an irritating result not only for the philosophical layman. Suppose there were 512 versions of group theory or 512 versions of thermo-dynamics. What is called for, it seems, is a reasonably small number of canonical statements of versions of realism and anti-realism. Formalization may help (a) to formulate this set of agreed upon theories in a well-understood language and (b) to explore the conceptual content and the logical consequences of these theories.

(ii) An example from epistemology is a theory (family) called doxastic voluntarism. It is not clear what the exact statement of this theory is. Sometimes it is said that doxastic voluntarism is the claim that some (or all?) our beliefs are subject to the will. Sometimes the question is raised whether the world forces beliefs upon doxastic subjects or not. Other authors discuss doxastic voluntarism by way of focusing on the notion of control about beliefs. A typology of kinds of control is developed in terms of basic, non-basic, immediate, direct, indirect, wide, and narrow control. Some authors hold that basic control over beliefs is psychologically impossible, whereas other authors claim that ascriptions of basic control over beliefs are false for conceptual reasons, that it is logically impossible to have such control over beliefs. Still another way of approaching the problems discussed under the banner of doxastic voluntarism and anti-voluntarism is inquiring whether belief formation or belief acquisition is a sort of action. Is a sentence like "John acquires the belief that Jim is guilty of theft." an action report? Voluntarism is also discussed in terms of deciding to believe. Are there ways of deciding to believe corresponding to distinct kinds of control over beliefs? Unfortunately, at the moment there is no canonical terminology, no agreed upon language of doxastic voluntarism. I must admit that I find the kinds-of-control terminology very unfortunate. I believe that formal methods may help to clarify the issues under consideration. It has often been emphasized that arguments against doxastic voluntarism may be used to argue against or even refute deontological conceptions of epistemic justification, the idea that an agent α is justified in believing that P if α is permitted to believe that P. In my view, the development of a multi-modal logic is required to obtain a precise theory and clear understanding of the notions involved and their interaction. What is needed is a modal logic of possibility, necessity, agency, belief, and deontic notions. In the language of such a multi-modal logic, possibility and impossibility claims about seeing to it that an agent believes something and claims about permissions to believe receive a clear meaning.

What example(s) from your work illustrates the role formal methods can play in philosophy?

I shall give two examples, which both concern work of other philosophers as well as my own work. The *first* example is not a very technical result, but it is to some extent typical of the role formal methods can play in philosophy, because it reflects the tension between capturing solid or deeply entrenched pre-theoretical intuitions on the one hand and shaping our every-day beliefs and general convictions on the other hand. Is it possible that an agent is responsible for the actions of another (single or collective) agent? It seems that our pre-theoretical beliefs concerning this question are not quite clear. Parents can be held or made responsible, it appears, for the actions of their children. Coaches of football teams can be held responsible for the performances of their teams etc. I believe that in order to better understand what the conceptual content of such responsibility attributions is, it is helpful to express these claims using a language of a deontic logic of agency. A promising candidate is the language of the seeing-to-it-that (stit) theory of Belnap, Perloff and Xu (*Facing the Future*, Oxford UP, 2001) extended by deontic modalities. This formalization helps, for example, to obtain an understanding of sentences such as the following:

(A) Agent α sees to it that β sees to it that P.

(B) Agent α ought to see to it that β sees to it that P.

(C) Agent α ought to see to it that it is not the case that β sees to it that P.

(D) Agent α ought to see to it that β refrains from seeing to it that P.

Suppose that α and β are distinct agents. In stit theory the independence of agents from each other is expressed by a condition on semantical models that makes sure that α cannot see to it that β sees to something. (This holds true for the achievement and deliberative seeing-to-it-that modal operators.) The sentence (A) therefore is unsatisfiable if α and β are independent of each other. Assuming the idea that *ought implies can* in the semantics of 'α ought to see to it that', it follows that sentence (B) is unsatisfiable if α and β are independent of each other. In stit theory it has been suggested that a sentence P is agentive for α just in case P may be usefully paraphrased as 'α sees to it that P'. A negated sentence 'It is not the case that β sees to it that P.' does not pass this test. In contrast to this, the sentence 'β refrains from seeing to it that P.' is agentive for α. Another guiding idea of stit theory is the so-called:

RESTRICTED COMPLEMENT THESIS. *A variety of constructions concerned with agents and agency – including deontic statements, imperatives, and statements of intention, among others – must take agentives as their complements.* (Belnap, Perloff and Xu, 2001, p. 13).

If this idea is taken seriously, as I think it should be, sentence (C) is not well-formed (or not interpretable) and sentence (D) is unsatisfiable if α and β are independent of each other. What are we to conclude from these observations? As already said, there are at least two perspectives available. The unsatisfiability observations may be taken to appropriately reflect or reveal pre-theoretical intuitions, or they may be seen as clarifying or even correcting common sense beliefs. In this case, both perspectives result in good news for the formal theory applied. Yes, it may be the case that an agent α sees to it that another agent β brings it about that something is the case, but then the agents are not independent of each other, perhaps because α has deprived β of some of the options β would have available in the absence of α. If the formal analysis is extended to the notion of responsibility, it turns out that agents cannot be responsible for the actions of other independent agents, but they can well be responsible for other independent agents being responsible, and such responsibility for responsibility may justify blame, praise, and other sanctions.

The *second* example takes up the earlier remarks on realism and anti-realism. Anti-realists with respect to meaning hold that the meaning of an expression is given with rules for the correct use of the expression. What exactly this (or related) claims may mean and imply can be elaborated in many ways, but to obtain a solid understanding it may be extremely useful to make all the relevant notions precise. What exactly is a rule? What exactly does it mean that a rule captures the correct use of an expression? It seems extremely difficult, if not just hopeless, to precisely define these notions for a natural language and thereby to obtain what is nowadays called a proof-theoretic semantics for the entire natural language under consideration. The earliest work that I am aware of on the proof-theoretic semantics of a formal language is Franz von Kutschera's work on the "Gentzen semantics" for intuitionistic logic and Nelson's constructive logic with strong negation. The meaning constituting rules are introduction rules in Gentzen's sequent calculus, and in order to make sure that the sequent rules for a logical connective are correct rules of use, the rules must have a certain shape that guarantees cut-elimination. I have applied these ideas and techniques to substructural subsystems of intuitionistic logic, constructive logic with strong negation and to certain modal logics. The approach allows semantical completeness and functional completeness results with respect to a proof-theoretic semantics and thereby reveals the feasibility in principle of an anti-realistic conception of meaning. This successful application of certain formal methods does not (and is not, of course, meant to) refute realism, but it provides a deeper understanding of the idea of meaning as use. It does not supplant prosaic philosophical analysis, but it supplements it.

Before I come to the next question, let me make clear that I do not intend to suggest that the application of formal methods is bound to lead to epistemic gain. Trivial or bad applications cannot be ruled out.

What is the proper role of philosophy in relation to other disciplines?

This is not an easy question. There exist so many other disciplines. Does philosophy play a single role with respect to any other discipline; the same abstract role in relation to, say, sociology as well as to physics or biology? In view of answers that have been given to this question in the literature, it is, perhaps, appropriate to say what in my view philosophy is *not*: It is not an auxiliary discipline. It is not a servant or slave of the other sciences. Of course, there are philosophies of other subjects: the philosophy of chemistry, the philosophy of biology, the philosophy of mathematics, etc. Philosophers of mathematics investigate, among other things, the epistemology, the ontology, and the methodology of mathematics, that is, the so-called Foundations of Mathematics. In the same way the philosophy of biology is concerned with the foundations of biology. Nevertheless philosophy is a discipline that is not exhausted by foundational studies of such a kind. It is an independent discipline of its own. It investigates many problems that are not problems of any particular science other than philosophy. Philosophy clarifies the foundations of other disciplines, but it has its specific problems: What are the truth conditions of knowledge ascriptions? What are the truth conditions of obligation ascriptions? What is a logical system? Is there a logic of imagination? And so on.

What do you consider the most neglected topics and/or contributions in late 20th century philosophy?

A neglected topic of philosophy in the late 20th century was, certainly, the Paradox of Knowability. It is now known that this paradox has been devised by Alonzo Church. After its publication in Frederic Fitch's paper "A logical analysis of some value concepts" (*Journal of Symbolic Logic* 28 (1963)) it was re-discovered in the late 1970s, and for quite a while it seemed that the Fitch-Paradox was an idiosyncratic subject of discussion between Timothy Williamson and Neil Tenant. Only at the beginning of the 21st century the significance and the challenge of the Paradox of Knowability to anti-realism have been widely recognized.

Another sort of neglected topic is connexive logic. It is well-known that Aristotle's syllogistic comprises inferences that are not classically valid under the standard translation into predicate logic. The most famous example is, perhaps, the inference from "Every P is Q" to "Some Ps are Qs":

$$\frac{\forall x(P(x) \to Q(x))}{\exists x(P(x) \land Q(x))} \qquad (15.1)$$

This inference has some plausibility in everyday life, because in everyday communication we usually do not quantify over the empty restrictor class. If we assume that the interpretation of P is empty, there is hardly any reason to assume that every P is Q, but if the interpretation of P is non-empty, (15.1) is a valid inference.

The schematic inference (15.1) cannot be consistently added as a rule to a proof system for classical predicate logic, as is obvious from the following instance of (15.1):

$$\frac{\forall x((P(x) \land \sim P(x)) \to Q(x))}{\exists x((P(x) \land \sim P(x)) \land Q(x))} \qquad (15.2)$$

The premise of (15.2) is classically valid, whereas the conclusion is classically unsatisfiable. In classical logic, inference (15.1) is, of course, interchangeable with

$$\frac{\forall x(P(x) \to Q(x))}{\exists x \sim (P(x) \to \sim Q(x))} \qquad (15.3)$$

Storrs McCall pointed out that in a system of connexive logic (15.3) is a valid inference. This is obviously the case in the quantified connexive logic QC, because there $\sim(A \to B) \leftrightarrow (A \to \sim B)$ is an axiom, and both the double-negation law and the Replacement Theorem for provably equivalent formulas hold. One might thus suggest that statements of the form "Some Ps are Qs" ought to be translated not as $\exists x(P(x) \land Q(x))$ but as $\exists x \sim (P(x) \to \sim Q(x))$, which in the system QC is equivalent to $\exists x(P(x) \to Q(x))$. Inference (3) then amounts to an instance of

$$\frac{\forall x R(x)}{\exists x R(x)} \tag{15.4}$$

which is valid if the familiar assumption of non-empty domains is made. The key step to validating inference (15.3) is defining negated implications $\sim (A \to B)$ as true iff $A \to \sim B$ is true. This equivalence may well reflect certain pre-theoretic intuitions about the meaning of implication and negation. What is perhaps more interesting is that the connexive understanding of negated implications suggests the question: "What is the correct constructive interpretation of false implications?", and then "What is constructive falsity?", "What is a constructive logic?"

What are the most important open problems in philosophy and what are the prospects for progress?

The open problems abound. What is a constructive logic? Is it possible to decide to believe, and, if so, how is deciding to believe to be modelled? Is there one correct logic, or should, in view of uncountably many logical systems, logical monism be abandoned? What is the role of the notion of truth in explanation compared with the role of the notion of information? More generally, what are relevant epistemic values and how are they inter-related? Among the epistemic values that may be considered are:

- consistency,
- non-triviality,
- simplicity,
- truth,
- justification,
- coherence,
- informativity,
- constructivity,
- tractability,
- explanatory power,
- problem-solving capacity.

Does or should an increase of constructivity lead to an increase of coherence? There is a rich inventory of problems and questions in this area that invite the application of formal methods and models.

One lesson to be learned from the 20th century philosophy of science is that progress is not always and perhaps even rarely cumulative; that it comes with changes of points of views, re-interpretations of terms, with partial or radical replacements of old theories and 'world-views'. Moreover, problem-solving is not a purely quantitative affair, as obviously some problems are more relevant than others. Thus, also the question about prospects for progress in philosophy is a quite difficult one. Naively speaking, I tend to believe that the prospects for progress are bright, at least if the expectations are not illusory. The application of formal methods admits mathematical results, but philosophical insights are, I am afraid, typically conditional. If certain premises are accepted, if the use of certain principles in the meta-theory is consensus, if particular ontological and methodological assumptions are shared, *then* one is committed to various consequences. The paradoxes – understood as ranging from derivations of inconsistency from (initially) plausible assumptions to inferences of perplexing or simply unwanted conclusions from (seemingly) innocuous premises – have always been one driving force of philosophical research. In recent decades much progress has been made in paradox analysis and in the treatment of paradoxes. The development of paraconsistent logics has challenged the standard attitude towards the semantical paradoxes, and the Curry-Paradox has played a role in the investigation of substructural logics. There has been progress in logic and in formal philosophy, and hence in philosophy. I see no reason why there should cease to be progress in philosophy in the future, except for extra-scientific reasons.[1]

---

[1] I have tried to keep this text in an interview-style. Therefore, I have refrained from giving detailed references. I would like to thank Vincent F. Hendricks and John Symons for their invitation to contribute to this volume.

16
Dag Westerståhl

Professor of Theoretical Philosophy
Department of Philosophy
Göteborg University, Sweden

Why were you initially drawn to formal methods?

I began with mathematics, attracted to the beauty and abstractness of its methods, but was drawn into philosophy partly because of the more directly perceptible human interest of the questions it posed. But my first weeks at the philosophy department in Göteborg convinced me that there was no real conflict between the two. My first class was an elementary logic course given by Per Lindström. It went at lightning speed; after a few lessons he had already reached Gödel's theorems. The students, including myself, understood little of the details, but I could still see that this was extremely fascinating stuff, that you could actually use mathematical methods to *prove* facts that were highly relevant to understanding human thinking, knowledge, and language. I decided it was worth learning those methods, and the fascination from that first class is still with me (I should add that some of it was due to Lindström's remarkable way of teaching: rapid, intensive, nervous, he was chain-smoking and completely absorbed in the subject.). Lindström, who later became my supervisor, was then in the process of arriving at his famous characterization theorems for first-order logic, another great example of mathematical methods leading to philosophically interesting results. The Göteborg philosophy department in that period was a great place to be for a young student vacillating between mathematics and philosophy.

What example(s) from your work illustrates the role formal methods can play in philosophy?

The best examples are a few celebrated results, like Gödels's theorems or Turing's analysis of the notion of an algorithm, that forever changed the way we think about truth, proof, and computation. But in fact formal methods apply on a larger even if more modest scale throughout philosophy. For one thing, they remind us that precision and clarity are virtues, and that clearly expressed hypotheses have equally clear consequences, that may be studied by these methods. The insights gained in this way are sometimes not sensational or even deep, but they are still insights. To be sure there is a movement in philosophy, to a great deal inspired by Wittgenstein, which denies that precision is beneficial or even that explanation is a task of philosophy (Wittgenstein, as is well known, could never bring himself to understand Gödel's results.). I don't want to claim that formal methods are always fruitful, or deny that insights, perhaps also deep ones, may be arrived at in other ways. But I believe it is a fundamental mistake to oppose formal methods to others in philosophy, or to relegate them to a small corner where logicians play.

For my own part, I have been impressed by the extent to which an exact study of language is possible. In a sense it should not be surprising that immensely complex yet systematically built structures like the syntax and semantics of human languages are amenable to, and sometimes require, study by mathematical methods. Still it was a revelation to many people when Chomsky showed in the 1950's how automata theory could be applied to syntax. And it was a revelation to me that methods already available from model theory could be directly and fruitfully applied to central linguistic areas, such as the study of quantifier expressions. In large part it was via Jon Barwise and Johan van Benthem that this insight dawned upon me. Through the work of them and many others I think we now know a great deal more about how these important expressions behave. All in all the study of (generalized) quantifiers in natural language has been a happy marriage between formal or logical methods and, in this case, linguistics and philosophy. In our recent book *Quantifiers in Language and Logic* (Oxford University Press, 2006), Stanley Peters and I try to summarize, assess, and develop further some of that knowledge.

Let me illustrate with a few examples (each of them discussed in our book), noting again that these are not meant to seem striking or deep; rather they are deliberately chosen to exemplify the 'day-to-day use' of formal methods. A linguistic example comes from so-called *polarity items*, words only allowed in 'negative contexts' (alternatively, 'positive' ones), like "ever" or "yet." The linguist wants to find a rule for the distribution of these. This requires a definition of 'negative context,' a notion which turns out to have not so much to do with explicit negation but rather with *monotonicity*, a concept familiar from mathematics. Using various specialized forms of monotonicity fairly good generalizations of the rather complex linguistic data have been found. This is so far standard theorizing, though with logical tools. But logic can contribute further. A hypothesis of the form "Words in class C occur only in contexts with monotonicity property M" should be tested against new examples. Finding such is the linguist's task, but logic might also provide a succinct and exact characterization of the M contexts. This may in turn significantly limit and guide the search for examples, perhaps leading to a revision of the hypothesis. Etc.

For a philosophical example, consider the notion of a *logical constant*. There are strong intuitions that certain words, like "and," "or," "every," behave in a significantly different way from most other words. Indeed they are logical constants in standard logics, but why these, and what is it that singles them out? This calls for careful conceptual analysis, which has proved to be non-trivial, but logic itself can offer some assistance. To take just one example, the 'topic neutrality' that appears to be a central part of the idea of logicality can be captured by various *invariance* conditions, familiar from model theory. The (sometimes drastic) effects of standard invariance conditions was studied in the early 1980s, but recent work by van Benthem, Feferman, Bonnay and others has started to explore new and stronger versions of such conditions. I am not saying that results along these lines necessarily provide clear-cut and simple answers to the philosophical question (for one thing, the idea that they could might strike some as inherently circular), but I do think they are indispensable for anyone who attempts a serious analysis of the notion of a logical constant.

A more difficult example concerns the idea of *expressive power*. Intuitions about what can or cannot be said by certain linguistic means, or in a certain language, are often strong, but also vague and without secure foundation. In particular, a claim about *non*-expressibility ought to be supported not on empirical grounds (which may fail due to lack of means or imagination) but by some sort of principled proof. A first step is to focus on *relative* expressibility in terms of what can be *translated* from one language into another. But the notion of (correct or adequate) translation is itself in need of elucidation. The issue concerns both translation between natural languages, and *formalization*, i.e. translation into a formal language. There is ample prospect for a successful use of formal methods in this area. Moreover, given that suitable notions of translation can be made precise, there is the possibility to transfer certain (non-)expressibility theorems from model theory to facts about natural languages. One has to be careful about the conditions for such a transfer to succeed, but when it does, the result is that expressibility claims previously founded on vague intuition and perhaps a few examples may be conclusively established (or refuted).

A final and partly methodological example is *compositionality*. Almost every linguist or philosopher of language has a strong opinion about the 'principle of compositionality' – the claim that the meaning of a complex expression is determined by the meanings of its parts and the mode of composition. But it is striking how these opinions differ. Some find the principle empirical and true, others empirical and false, yet others see it as an essential characteristic of human language, whereas some claim it is trivial and/or empty. It is somewhat embarrassing that such an apparently central issue in meaning theory is the object of so much disagreement. Clearly, much confusion pertains to this area, which seems ripe for philosophical clarification. And it seems equally clear that formal methods are going to be indispensable in order to make progress here. Such progress has already begun, but more remains to be done.

What is the proper role of philosophy in relation to other disciplines?

I see philosophy as critical and argued *reflection* over practically any field of human endeavor, and thus in particular over any academic discipline. No doubt it is useful for any discipline to step back, from time to time, and reflect on itself. Existing philosophy can help, but sometimes it is rather the scientists or workers in that discipline who need to resort to, or invent, a philosophical 'stance.' In addition, philosophy has had the historic role of posing new questions, questions which at times have generated new disciplines (think of logic, and psychology, for recent examples).

A *fortiori*, the boundaries between philosophy and certain disciplines are sometimes hard to draw or even nonexistent. But the idea that philosophy is the most basic discipline is essentially correct, I think, as long as this is not taken to entail that philosophers have all the answers. What they (sometimes) have are *methods*, including formal ones, for possibly finding answers, or at least posing fruitful questions that may lead to answers.

All of this should be obvious and uncontroversial. That there is still controversy about the role of philosophy may be due to scientists' unwillingness to admit that non-specialists could have anything of value to say about their field, or to philosophers behaving as if they know more about a special field than they in fact do. Both attitudes are psychologically understandable but neither is theoretically very interesting.

What are the most important open problems in philosophy and what are the prospects for progress?

Rather than making a list I will mention just one set of problems, concerning precisely the use of formal methods. A striking feature of modern logic is the extraordinary *variety* of logics, formal languages, proof systems, etc. that have been invented in recent times and applied successfully to the study of language, computation, time, knowledge, information, communication, morals, and what not. The logician's toolbox has indeed proved unexpectedly useful. But this raises an old problem: What *is* logic? Is it essentially a box of technical tools that can be used to *describe* (and hence understand) human forms of reasoning? One imagines how Frege would turn in his grave at such a characterization. Didn't the success story of modern logic also begin with the realization that logic is not the study of how we *in fact* think or reason but rather of how we *must* think if we are to reason *correctly*? Surely there is something fundamentally right in Frege's anti-psychologistic conception of logic (as concerned with the laws of truth, not the laws of 'holding true'). Yet many modern logicians seem to embrace without qualms a psychological, or at least descriptive/instrumental, view of logic.

A different but related problem, also stemming from the rich variety of present-day logics, is what we are to make of situations when such logics seem to *conflict* with each other, as, for example, in the (at least apparent) conflict between classical and intuitionistic logic (not to mention logics that reject the law of contradiction). It seems to me that it is time for logic to step back and assess these issues. At least it is time for philosophers and philosophically minded logicians to do that. Perhaps there is no real conflict between Frege's view of logic and the modern development. Or perhaps a radically new perspective on logic has emerged, but if so it is one that needs to be formulated. To sort out this issue would be not only of theoretical interest, but would help us who like to use formal methods in philosophy better understand what we are actually doing. This project has not been given much attention recently, at least not by logicians, so the prospects of progress are good. Who knows, formal methods may again prove useful in the process.

17

Jan Wolenski

Professor of Philosophy

Jagiellonian University, Cracow, Poland

Why were you initially drawn to formal methods?

I studied law (1956–1963) and philosophy (1960–1964), both at the Jagiellonian University. At that time, every student of law (as well as of most other faculties at Polish universities) had an obligatory class in logic. The courses at the legal faculty were conducted by Professor Władysław Wolter. He was an excellent lecturer. Although he was not a logician (in fact, he specialized in penal law), his lectures were very competent and attracted me to logic. My other path to logic was via legal theory, in which I became interested at the very beginning of my studies. At so-called exercises (auxiliary classes to lectures) we also considered the methodological status of jurisprudence, in particular, of doctrinal studies of law. I was asked to prepare a report about one scholarly paper about this topic. The author referred to Tarski's distinction between object language and meta-language. I went to the library of the Department of Philosophy, asked for the relevant issue of *Przegląd Filozoficzny* (*Philosophical Review*) and read the quoted Tarski paper, namely "The Establishment of Scientific Semantics". The whole issue (vol. 39, number 1, 1936) contains three other papers, namely Tarski's on the concept of logical consequence, Kokoszyńska's on the relation of syntax and semantics and Fleck's on the concept of scientific observation. I read all the mentioned papers. Of course, I did not realize what was their real quality and importance. Nevertheless, since I was very excited by this encounter with philosophy, I decided to visit the library of the Philosophy Department every morning in order to read other volumes of *Przegląd Filozoficzny*. The instructor in legal theory observed the growth my philosophical interests and recommended to me some books of Ajdukiewicz, Czeżowski and Kotarbiński, the leading members of the Lvov-Warsaw School. In a bookshop I found some volumes of *Studia Logica*, bought them and began to read.

Very soon I realized that my logical knowledge was by far insufficient to understand most papers in *Studia Logica*. This was the main motivation to take philosophy as the subject of regular studies. Unfortunately, the teaching of logic was not particularly intensive in the philosophy program in Cracow at that time. Professor Kazimierz Pasenkiewicz, who taught us logic, had health problems and often cancelled his classes. Philosophy was dominated by Professor Roman Ingarden, a student of Husserl, who was not very friendly to logic. Professor Izydora Dąmbska, a student of Twardowski, had courses and seminars in philosophy of science and semantics, but they were rather elementary. The program of formal logic was modeled on Mostowski's textbook published in 1948, but omitted most metalogical problems. The situation changed in 1962, when Stan Surma appeared in Cracow and began very intensive teaching of logic. Unfortunately, I was too busy with my master's thesis in law in order to fully profit from this new situation. Thus, I must say that I learned logic by myself, as an autodidact with all the consequences of this. On the one hand, I read very much, but my learning was not guided by a specialist.

One additional autobiographical feature should be mentioned. Relatively early, still as a student of the 3rd year, I was promised to be appointed in the Department of Legal Theory. Professor Kazimierz Opałek, the head of this unit, invited me to participate in weekly scientific meetings. I regarded this as a great honor. Various methodological problems were discussed very often at these meetings. However, one question was continuous, namely the logic of norms. I decided to specialize in the borderline of legal theory, philosophy and logic. This dominated my work in 1963–1979. I wrote my doctoral dissertation about the relation of legal theory to philosophy, taking Hart's jurisprudence as an example. More specifically, I investigated how Hart's idea of jurisprudence displays ordinary-language philosophy. My habilitation concerned the logical problems of legal interpretation. In 1979 I finished a book about analytical legal philosophy. I also worked in the history of logic. I moved to the Technical University in Wrocław in 1979. Since I was appointed as a philosopher, my links with legal theory became weaker. This resulted in the growth of my purely philosophical interests.

My biography was decisive for forming my idea of what are

formal methods and how they should be applied in philosophy. I was (and am) heavily influenced by the Polish tradition. In general, I share Łukasiewicz's view that although philosophy is not reducible to logic, logical language is optimal for expressing philosophical ideas, because, pace Leśniewski, logic is a formal exposition of intuition. Of course, not everything which is philosophically important, is logically expressible. This fact limits the scope of logical philosophy. However, one additional remark is in order here. Speaking about logical expressibility or logical philosophy we can have two things in mind. Firstly, we can claim that philosophy, as every other intellectual human activity, is to fulfill elementary logical virtues, like clarity, systematic order, etc. To appeal to Łukasiewicz once again, logic is the morality of thought and speech. I follow this postulate. Although not everything is formally expressible, every use of language, philosophical or not, must be logically transparent. Most problems discussed by Heidegger and Camus do not fall under logical languages, but the latter speaks clearly, while the former obscurely. Secondly, the role of logic in philosophy consists in providing devices for the analysis of philosophical concepts. And this job of logic in philosophy interests me in a particular way.

My work on Hart convinced me that the contrast of ordinary and formal language is usually exaggerated. Thus, we should look for a compromise between constructivism (formalism, logicism, etc.; of course, these labels have nothing to do with positions in the foundations of mathematics) and descriptivism (ordinary language philosophy, informalism, etc.). I believe that philosophical logic, which envisages various formal systems, provides instruments for studying various language-games and thereby tools for a successful analysis of various philosophical concepts, including the most fundamental ones, like, being, existence, knowledge, obligation, etc. However, applications of logical or formal theories to philosophy have a feature which is often overlooked. I will demonstrate the point by the following example. Some people argue that the uncertainty principle (UC) in quantum mechanics implies indeterminism. This is a mistake. This principle, expressed by the equation $\Delta p \times \Delta q \geq h$ (Δp – the uncertainty of position, Δq – the uncertainty of momentum, h – the Planck constant), concerns the relation between parameters that characterize the mechanical state of an elementary particle. Since UC says nothing about determinism or indeterminism, it cannot imply any of these conflicting philosophical views. In order to derive something philosophical from UC, one must do some preparatory work, for example, define determinism in some way. Heisenberg, who formulated UC did such a job; he definied determinism as the view that the future states of mechanical objects are uniquely predicted on the basis of their past states. This definition as a supplementary premise entails, together with UC, indeterminism. The situation is this: We have a formal theory, logical or mathematical, and we have a philosophical problem. Now we claim that we are able to capture or even solve this problem by using a formal scheme. I claim that this task is realizable only if this formal scheme is embedded into a philosophical language. Usually, this step involves many philosophical traditions, for example, in thinking about determinism and indeterminism. I am not afraid to say that embedding formal tools into philosophical language consists in looking for a hermeneutical factor expressible in a formal way. Returning to Leśniewski's earlier quoted opinion about a formal exposition of intuition, we can also say that logical tools expose hermeneutics present in philosophical views. According to Ajdukiewicz, translations of philosophical theses into logic are paraphrases with an unavoidable hermeneutic flavor. I am inclined to speak about the interpretative philosophical consequences of logical or formal schemes. Thus, philosophical analysis does not consist in deriving purely logical consequences from formal items, but in looking for consequences mediated by a given hermeneutics. Needless to say, this view leads to scepticism with respect to possibility of ultimate solutions of philosophical problems. However, I do not think that this situation is desperate. In my opinion, every epoch invents its own tools for expressing prevalent philosophical ideas and this fact constitutes progress in philosophy. Logic became a philosophical instrument in the 20th century and perhaps it is more important than hopeless in searching for ultimate solutions.

What example(s) from your work illustrates the role formal methods can play in philosophy?

Of course, there are many very good examples. Łukasiewicz's analysis of determinism is my favorite case, although I do not agree that fatalism follows from the principle of bivalence. However, his way of using logical tools for the analysis of the problem of determinism was brilliant. Although I am perfectly conscious that my own work is of a secondary importance, I feel myself allowed by the editors to refer to my own attempts. I can mention (1) my analysis of the distinctions of analytic / synthetic and *a priori* / *a posteriori* in *Handbook of Epistemology*, ed. by I. Niiniluoto, M. Sintonen and myself, Kluwer Academic Publishers, Dordrecht (the chapter "Analytic vs. Synthetic and A Priori vs. A Posteriori") – this analysis employs various metamathematical results; (2) my reconstruction of the semantic definition of truth as a philosophical theory (many papers, and a monograph in preparation) – I try to show extensively how Tarski's ideas clarify the traditional advantages and troubles of the classical theory of truth; (3) my analysis of the concept of logic in "First-Order Logic: (Philosophical) Pro and Contra," in *First-Order Logic Revisited*, ed. by V.F. Hendricks, F. Neuhaus, S.A. Pedersen, U. Scheffler and H. Wansing, Logos Verlag, Berlin 2004 – I argue for the first-order thesis taking into account the properties traditionally attached to logic.

What is the proper role of philosophy in relation to other disciplines?

My opinion is that philosophy provides neither premises for other sciences nor consists of the consequences of scientific theories. I argued for the second thesis above, but the first seems to me obvious. In general, the scientists abstain from basing their solutions on philosophical assumptions; otherwise, we have pathological situations, like the Galileo trial, Aryan physics or Marxist genetics. Speaking formally, the consequences of philosophical statements belong to philosophy, but consequences of scientific statements belong to science; I agree with Wittgenstein that philosophy is above or below science, but never beside it. Using a workable distinction, philosophy does not belong to the context of justification in science, although it can play an important role in the context of discovery; the heuristic role of philosophy in science is particularly well demonstrated by the Einstein/Bohr controversy in the foundations of quantum mechanics. This view about philosophy does not diminish its cultural role. Philosophy forms a part of scientific culture at all times and cannot be erased from the intellectual life of any epoch.

17. Jan Wolenski

What do you consider the most neglected topics and/or contributions in late 20th century philosophy? What are the most important open problems in philosophy and what are the prospects for progress?

I am always puzzled by such questions. Although I have great sympathy for logical empiricism, the philosophical cutting knife of this position seems to me very improper. In other words, I am against any *a priori* and general verdict about what philosophy is, what its progress consists in, etc. I have my favorite philosophy, that is, analytic in its formal dressing, but I am very far from condemning other metaphilosophical positions, unless I can show their weakness, according to my own standard. Thus, if I say that Heidegger or Derrida are obscure, I add at once that I am guided by my own preferences. I am strongly inclined to philosophical pluralism. I have no feeling that contemporary philosophy has neglected some problems. I recall that not every kind of philosophy is equally suitable for all possible philosophical problems. Formal or logical philosophy has difficulties with copying philosophical anthropology, but it would difficult to expect that existentialism could be effective with respect to the philosophy of mathematics. Of course, there are more and less fashionable problems at a given time. For example, philosophy of mind became recently very much in vogue, but that is probably caused by the development of artificial intelligence. Bioethics is another example connected with various biological experiments. In general, I trust the natural development of philosophy and think that it should not be artificially accelerated or slowed. One thing which comes to my mind in this context is that the division of philosophy into analytic and continental is a mistake and should be abandoned.

18
John Woods

Director of The Abductive Systems Group and
Charles S. Peirce Professor of Logic
University of British Columbia, Canada / King's College London, UK

Why were you initially drawn to formal methods?

An early philosophical moment occurred when, at age four, I was saying my bed-time prayers. 'God bless Mummy and Daddy and [sisters] Barbie and Joanie.' I bade the Almighty, 'and make me a good boy after a while.' Years later I would discover my Augustinian sensibility in the entreaty by the author of the *Confessions* that God render him chaste, but not now. Two years later, our Grade One teacher asked what we thought enabled Our Lord to perform the miracle of the loaves and fishes. Up snapped my hand: 'Because He is magic!' 'No, no,' admonished Sister Anne, 'it is because He is *God*.' Thus was I introduced to the dissatisfaction of vacuous truths. A third episode involved my art teacher, Mrs. Harvey, who offered instruction on Saturday mornings. She would give me a lesson in the appearance-reality distinction. 'You can't get snow right with white paint,' she insisted. 'How could this be?' I wondered. 'Isn't white the colour of snow?' 'Because,' Mrs. Harvey replied, 'when you see snow you always see more than its colour. You also see shadow. So you don't paint what the *colour* of snow is; you paint what snow *looks* like.'

As a First-year student at the University of Toronto, I had the good and bad fortune to have had as my philosophy teacher Emil Fackenheim, one of his era's foremost students of Jewish philosophy, and a commanding figure in Continental philosophy. His lectures on philosophy were a delight, but when, towards the end of the year, we switched to Angus Sinclair's slim little volume on syllogistic logic, disaster loomed. Professor Fackenheim hadn't the faintest interest in Aristotle's logic – never mind Whitehead and

Russell's – and did nothing whatever to motivate it. His lectures were carbon copies of the tinder-dry chapters of Sinclair's text. It was a pretty bleak four or so weeks. The first thing I noticed about the syllogistic was that its categorical vocabulary was laughably unrepresentative. Singular sentences could be accommodated only artificially, and molecular sentences couldn't be accommodated at all. When I complained of this to a Fourth-year philosophy house-mate, he referred me in the first instance to *On Interpretation* and, in the second, to the *Prior Analytics*. In *On Interpretation*, Aristotle asserts (but does not prove) that anything stateable in Greek is stateable without relevant loss in the language of categorical propositions. I was struck by this. If this audacious (and admittedly implausible) claim were true, the language of the syllogistic wasn't unrepresentative after all. The four types of categorical proposition could bear the whole expressive load. The *Prior Analytics* contained an even more striking revelation. Its perfectability thesis comes close to making the property of syllogisisty effectively recognizable. After some mulling over, I was able to see both the unproved thesis and the almost-proved thesis as setting out bold reductionist strategies, by virtue of which any argument whatever can be assessed in low finite time by quasi-mechanical methods. Of course, since the reductionist claim of *On Interpretation* isn't proved, the strategy is more promissory than realized. But the idea of it was there for all to see, and I was captivated by it.

The near-proof of the perfectability thesis turns on the manipulation of structure. In one sense of the word, it is a manipulation of form (notwithstanding that Aristotle had no *doctrine* of logical form). I began to see that considerations of form can bear essentially on the vaunted appearance-reality distinction. That every inapparent syllogism can be converted into an obvious syllogism cannot be proved except formally. And an argument that has the appearance of not being a syllogism may well instantiate a structure by virtue of which it is a syllogism in fact, and moreover a structure which, when manipulated in the right way, makes this fact apparent. It was not until my M.A. year in Toronto, that I saw the doctrine that grammatical form camouflages logical form upheld in Russell's lectures on Logical Atomism. I was chuffed no end that the idea embedded in my naïve reading of Aristotle's intent was vigorously championed by the likes of Russell.

By the end of that same year, I was to complete a course on the Philosophy of History given by William Dray. Professor Dray was then (the year was 1959) on the upswing of a large reputation as the slayer of the deductive-nomological model of explanation in historical contexts. After some early positivistic resistance on my part, I capitulated. I had learned another valuable lesson. It was that in attempting to explain historical explanation, Professor Hempel and his logical empiricist colleagues had appropriated an ill-considered theoretical model. When applied to historical explanation, the formal apparatus of D-N derivations was the wrong fit. I would later come to call this sort of thing "paradigm-creep", which is the assimilation of a subject-matter to an attractive, well-understood, but inappropriate theoretical model for it.

The following year I was a PhD student at the University of Michigan. Aside from some rigorous courses by Richard Cartwright, Michigan was agog over Oxford linguist analysis. When J.L. Austin died in 1960, the Department all but went into mourning. I thought at the time that a good deal of what passed for philosophy in the Philosophy-Without-Tears School (in Russell's pungent riposte) was pretty small beer. Even so, yet another important lesson could be learned from the example of the best practitioners of this movement (of whom Dray was one). It is that a formal theory can have all the metatheoretical virtues you like – soundness, completeness, the lot – and still give a bad account of its target notion. Of course, a philosophical theory cannot get started except as encoding the theorist's initial intuitions about the matter at hand. What Ordinary Language Philosophy got me to see was that raw intuitions that aren't carefully reflected on can end up poisoning the theory that attempts to preserve and build on them. This I would later call "the problem of immature data for theory."

The last of my youthful lessons about formal methods I learned from Jaakko Hintikka's *Knowledge and Belief*, which appeared in 1962, just as I was heading back to Toronto for my first academic appointment. I was greatly impressed with the idea that standard systems of modal logic might respond well to epistemic interpretations of $\Box$ and $\Diamond$. In Hintikka's approach, the logic of knowledge and belief is an epistemicization of Lewis' **S4**, which was a well-understood system of modal logic. The characteristic axiom of **S4** is "If $\vdash \Box\alpha$ then $\vdash \Box\Box\alpha$", which means in its epistemic variation that if x knows that α, x knows that he knows that α (the so-called KK-hypothesis). My first reaction was, in effect, to bring a charge of paradigm-creep against Hintikka. In order to get the formal apparatus of **S4** to fit the analysis of knowledge, the concept of knowledge is distorted beyond recognition. For, as I then thought and still do, the last thing that the ordinary concept of knowledge will dance to is the KK-hypothesis. But in a 1968 paper Hintikka claimed that the idea captured by his epistemic logic was indeed – once you think about it a bit – the intuitive concept of knowledge. So perhaps I myself had fallen prey to the immature data problem. The matter took on a further complication in a paper of two years later, where Hintikka suggested that a concept with such a lovely logic in the offing is one that is just begging to be changed in order to fit it. This was my first experience of the idea a good formal model might furnish reasons to redefine the target concept in ways that permit the model to engage it deeply. Some philosophers would call this "conceptual reconstruction."

I would later learn that the distinctions that I was dimly trying to sort out had been present in Kant all along. Kant distinguished between making concepts clear and making clear concepts. Making concepts clear is analysis and is, says Kant, the proper business of philosophy. Making clear concepts is synthesis and is, he says, the proper business of mathematics. Some two centuries later Quine would remind us that the divide between explication and stipulation cannot be drawn in a non-arbitrary way. This is Kant's distinction nearly enough; and Quine was calling attention to the fact that theoretical models that start out as explications of their target concepts can end up as stipulations of successor concepts, and that this is no bad thing. Carnap's distinction between internal and external questions was intended to make a similar point.

What example(s) from your work illustrates the role formal methods can play in philosophy?

Notwithstanding my initial reservations about Hintikka's epistemic adaptation of **S4**, I myself was up to the same sort of thing in 1974, when *The Logic of Fiction* appeared. After reviewing some approaches to the semantics of fictional discourse, I proposed a modal logic for fiction, pivoting on the fictive operator 'O', named after the Latin *olim* for "once upon a time." The negative parts of the book I still regard as successful. They show that some of the going formal paradigms are wrong for fiction. These include the theory of definite descriptions, free logics, supervaluational semantics and Meinongean semantics. My complaint, each time was to the effect that these formalizations produce unacceptable levels of paradigm-creep. The positive part of *The Logic of Fiction* fares less well. I wanted to keep the logic as mainstream as possible. For example, I crudely collapsed the problem of filling out a story with sentences not expressly contained in it (what Terence Parsons calls the problem of the maximum account) with the deductive closure of those contained sentences. Not only is this paradigm-creep in its own right, but some of the closure conditions admit of counterexamples.

Since the early 1970s, I have done a good deal of work on the logic of fallacious reasoning, for the first dozen years in collaboration with my former student, Douglas Walton. Together, Walton and I fashioned what came to be known as the Woods-Walton Approach. In it, we undertook to model this or that fallacy in some suitable-looking non-classical logic, of which then, and since, there was an *embarras de richesses*. We found that circularity could be blocked in Kripke structures of the sort devised for the completeness proof of modal intuitionist logic. We found that a suitable analysis of the part-whole relation, required for the elucidation of the fallacies of composition and division, was not forthcoming in set theory, or a Lesniewskian mereology, or a Suppes-Noll theory of bodies. But Tyler Burge's aggregation theory proved remarkably accommodating. Some members of the informal logic movement regretted the "logocentrism" of this approach. Some complained that it made the analysis of fallacious reasoning too difficult to teach to beginning students. As the years passed, Walton embraced a more dialectical approach to the fallacies, in which there is no inherent hostility to formal methods. I have undergone a more radical transformation. I have nothing against formal methods in fallacy theory, but I have come to the view that, when committed by individual agents, none of the standard examples of them is a fallacy after all. On the face of it, this is absurd. So a further brief word would be in order here, especially as it bears on the issue of paradigm creep.

The standard view among logicians is that when a piece of reasoning is invalid, or when it is inductively weak, then the reasoner has committed an error. Accordingly, among logically minded investigators of fallacious reasoning, the traditional view is that, virtually without exception, the fallacies commit the error of either invalidity (e.g., denying the antecedent) or inductive weakness (e.g., hasty generalization). It is worthy of note that logicians have achieved some degree of settled success in laying bare the logical structures of these two properties. The trouble is that they are *not* errors. Something is an error only in relation to the nature of his cognitive target and the attainment standards embedded in it.

If I want a proof of a theorem in topology, then truth-preservation is my goal, and validity is one of the standards for its attainment. If I want to determine the safety of a new drug for AIDS that my team and I are working on for the Department of Health, then experimental confirmation is my target and inductive strength is a standard for its attainment. But most of the reasoning that individuals engage in on the ground, including most of the *good* reasoning, is not motivated by such targets and is not held to such standards. We have it, then, that most good reasoning is neither valid nor inductively strong. But, if that is right, the fact that most of the fallacies are invalid or inductively weak moves underdetermines whether they are errors, which means in turn that it underdetermines whether they are fallacies. Of course, they might still be errors for reasons other than invalidity or inductive weakness. I doubt that this is so, but this is not the place to make that case. Suffice it to say that the hegemony of the logic of deductive consequence and of the logic of confirmation has badly influenced the theory of fallacious reasoning ever since its inception in the *Topics* and *On Sophistical Refutations*. This is paradigm-creep on a grand scale.

At present Dov Gabbay and I are writing our omnibus work, *A Practical Logic of Cognitive Systems*. The first two volumes, *Agenda Relevance* and *The Reach of Abduction* appeared in 2003 and 2005, and two others, on the logic of plausibility and the logic of fallacious reasoning (see just above) are scheduled for 2007 or early 2008. In these volumes, Gabbay and I take seriously the problems of immature data and paradigm-creep. Each book is broken into two parts. In part one we work up a detailed conceptual model of our target properties. The idea of converting immature intuitions into mature (or considered) intuitions, is an adaptation of Patrick Suppes' notion from the early 1960s of "models of data", except that Suppes was thinking of empirical data and we are thinking of conceptual data. The conceptual model is input for the formal model, which is the main business of part two. Our working hypothesis is that if the conceptual model is any good, it should stand a better than fair chance of being modeled formally. Of course, it goes without saying that often, in various respects, a conceptual model isn't able to be accommodated formally. When this happens, we have a methodological problem. It is the problem of finding a principled reason for "pinning the blame". Do we pin it on the conceptual model, arguing that it contains claims that can't be sanctioned formally? Or do we pin it on the formal model, arguing that it is powerless to recognize significant conceptual truths? Alternatively, do we allow the formal model to change the very concept which, left unchanged, cannot be captured by the formalism? Or do we tough it out and resist the impulse for conceptual change?

Gabbay and I are unable to see any general recipe for answering these questions. Instead, when they do arise, we attempt to deal with them on a case by case basis. Perhaps this is not methodologically ideal. But at least we point up the difficulties, and make some effort to deal with them (albeit, not always conclusively).

I will not speak for Dov, but I have come to think of the related issues of immature data, paradigm-creep and conceptual change as methodologically fundamental to philosophy. The Oxford crowd were wrong to think that formal methods in philosophy were, as such, excessively distorting. But they were right to warn us that there is more to a good formalization of a philosophically interesting concept than the metamathematical virtues of soundness and completeness, and the like.

What is the proper role of philosophy in relation to other disciplines?

Curiosity, detachment, generosity and humility. Philosophy has a natural tendency not to respect disciplinary borders. It seems always to be poking its nose into places where it is not wanted. It is true that much of the time the philosopher's interest is benign, and that what is sought is the clearing up of obscurities or the removal of ambiguities or inconsistencies in the host discipline. In nearly every case, however, this philosophical poaching leaves the host discipline unmarked. Instead, philosophical reflections upon it loop back and enrich philosophy itself. A case in point is the present state of philosophical reflection on Cognitive neuropsychology. Philosophy has not done much to make the science of this discipline better, but its cogitations have transformed both epistemology and philosophy of mind. So the first lesson to learn about the philosophy of X is that the first, and usually only, beneficiary is philosophy, not X.

What do you consider the most neglected topics and/or contributions in late 20th century philosophy?

I speak only for English-speaking countries. In those places in the past thirty years we have seen the near wholesale abandonment of non-analytic or "continental" philosophy to amateurs in departments of literature, education and law, who have no talent for it and who use its presumed lessons to validate some of the worst intellectual corruptions to have developed in non-totalitarian societies. Formal philosophers may disdain the methodological sloppiness of the likes of Heidegger and Merleau-Ponty. But philosophy is nothing without pregnant ideas. What we learn from the superb commentaries of analytically trained philosophers, such as Herbert Dreyfus on Heidegger and Dagfinn Føllesdall on Husserl, is that one can recover great ideas engendered by problematic methods. This takes us straight back to the "reconstructive" role of self-conscious rigour. Dreyfus' reconstruction of (part of) *Being and Time* may not be "pure wool" Heidegger, but it is wonderful philosophy.

Closer to home are the fundamentally important contributions of Stig Kanger to modal logic in the 20th century. Now that his *Collected Papers* have appeared with Kluwer (now Springer), a good many of his previously inaccessible papers on the modalities and other philosophical issues are available for the serious inspection that they richly deserve.

What are the most important open problems in philosophy and what are the prospects for progress?

Unlike the physical sciences, philosophy is a cyclical discipline, not a progressive one. Whatever the good to philosophy rendered by its formal methods, the best mark of progress can only be that of temporary respite from the agitations that drive philosophical enquiry. Philosophical problems subside not from having been solved, but rather from dialectical fatigue. They then lurk in their dormancy, awaiting revival at some later time. All questions in philosophy are open. Still leading the list are the Kantian three: the existence of God, the immortality of the soul, and freedom of will. Kant was an idealist *malgré lui*. Idealism will be the next big-box item to arise from its present dormancy.

About the Editors

Vincent F. Hendricks is Professor of Epistemology, Logic and Methodology and member of IIP — Institut Internationale de Philosophie. He is the author of many books including *Mainstream and Formal Epistemology, Thought$_2$ Talk, The Convergence of Scientific Knowledge, Feisty Fragments, Logical Lyrics* and *500 CC: Computer Citations*. Other books include *Self-Reference, Proof Theory, Probability Theory* and *Knowledge Contributors* and *New Waves in Epistemology*. Editor of *Synthese* and *Synthese Library* he is also the founder of ΦLOG—*The Network for Philosophical Logic and Its Applications*.

John Symons teaches philosophy at the University of Texas at El Paso and is an associate member of l'Institut d'Histoire et de Philosophie des Sciences et des Techniques, Université de Paris 1. In addition to numerous articles, he is the author of two books on Daniel Dennett's philosophy, *On Dennett* and *Daniel Dennett: Le Naturalisme en Chantier*. Other books include *Quantifiers, Questions and Quantum Physics: Essays on the Philosophy of Jaakko Hintikka* and *Logic, Epistemology and the Unity of Science*. Symons has edited *Synthese* and *Synthese Library* since 2002 and has represented Ireland in the Institut Internationale de Philosophie since 2004.

About Formal Philosophy

Formal Philosophy is a collection of short interviews based on 5 questions presented to some of the most influential and prominent scholars in formal philosophy. We hear their views on formal philosophy, its aim, scope, the future direction of philosophy and how their work fits in these respects.

> An interesting collection, and the website has excerpts of interviews with many well-known philosophers and logicians. The autobiographical remarks by Clark Glymour (Carnegie Mellon University) are especially entertaining, but also check out the excerpts from interviews with Dagfinn Føllesdal (Stanford / Oslo) discussing the relationship between philosophy and other disciplines; Wolfgang Spohn (Konstanz) reflecting on, as it were, the political economy of the discipline of philosophy over the last 50 years; and Patrick Suppes (Stanford) and Timothy Williamson (Oxford) on 'open problems' in philosophy.
>
> — **Brian Leiter**, *Leiter Reports*, November 11, 2005

WWW.FORMALPHILOSOPHY.COM
© 2005–6 Vincent F. Hendricks & John Symons

> What to put under the X-mas tree this year? Vincent F. Hendricks and John Symons' *Formal Philosophy*. A series of interviews with some of the top people in

formal philosophy the last decades, e.g., van Benthem, S. Haack, D. Føllesdal, J. Hintikka, P. Suppes and T. Williamson. If you want to read some abstracts of the interviews, why don't go here or maybe, if you want the book in time for Christmas, this is where you should go. Mine is already on its way.

— **Ole Thomassen Hjortland**, *Nothing of Consequence*, November 16, 2005

I just ran across Formal Philosophy, edited by Vincent Hendricks and John Symons (Automatic Press / VIP, 2005). It's a priced, printed book consisting of interviews with a large number of philosophers who use formal (i.e. logical and mathematical) methods in their work. What's interesting here is that the publisher has posted substantial excerpts from many of the interviews free online, presumably as an advertisement to help sell the book. Note how much larger these excerpts are than the Google Library snippets that have frightened some publishers into a litigious frenzy. There are probably many books like *Formal Philosophy* and publishers like Automatic Press / VIP. Of course there are also many books for which free online full-text coexists with a priced, print edition which helps boost its sales. This is just a reminder that Pat Schroeder and the AAP don't speak for all book publishers, just as Nick Taylor and the Authors Guild don't speak for all book authors.

— **Peter Suber**, *Open Access News*, November 17, 2005

What does the book achieve? First of all, it gives an impression of what formal philosophy is, not by definition but rather by examples indicating the range of formal philosophy. Second, it gives an impression of what kind of scientists are working in this field, what their motivations for doing formal philosophy are, and which or what kind of insights and results they have obtained and which methods they have developed or applied. Third, the book presents an interesting snapshot of intellectual history, and it is not for the least part that the latter aspect makes the book a very interesting reading.

— **Heinrich Wansing**, review in *Philosophical Books*, 2006

Formal Philosophy, in its sprawling and sometimes endearing way, captures the multiplicity of origin, aim and justification of the use of formal methods in philosophy. Whether philosophers come to formal methods reluctantly, forced to do so by the need for precision or by the nature of the problems studied, or with joy, sensing that abstract structures provide the key to understanding the world about us, they agree about the intellectual power afforded by such methods, and the pitfalls that surround them. Anyone interested in the methods of philosophy should read this book.

— **John Cantwell**, review in *Theoria*, 2007

It is for this reason that *Formal Philosophy* is a terrific book. Hendricks and Symons struck upon an ingenious method for getting giants in the field to talk freely about why formal philosophy is important, and how it should be done.

— **Gregory Wheeler**, review in *Philosophy of Science*, 2007

Index

a posteriori, 11, 138
a posteriorism, 80
a priori, 138
a priorism, 80
abortion, 79
abstract representational system, 38
abstraction, hypostatic, 107
action, 40, 49, 121
   coordinated, 3
   rational, 51
   report, 121
Adams, E., 39, 41
agency, 33, 120, 122
   metaphysics of, 78
agent, 51, 91, 122
   artificial, 84
   epistemic, 118
   multi-, 33
   rational, 3, 33
AIDS, 146
Ajdukiewicz, K., 135
algebra, 53, 105
Amsterdam, 120
Analysis, 23
analysis, 53
   classical, 1
analyticity, 103
anaphora, 96
ancestor, 83
Anderson, A., 94
anti-realism, 87, 95, 99, 120, 123
approximation, 113
architecture, 65

argument, 46
   Dutch Book, 49
   form, 47
   ontological, 46
   representation theorem, 49
   valid, 47
Aristotle, 4, 62, 125, 141
   On Interpretation, 142
   Prior Analytics, 142
arithmetic, 48, 62, 84, 105
Arló-Costa, H., 54
Arrow, K., 1
   impossibility theorem, 1
art, 65, 77
Artemov, S., 22, 86
artifact, 77
artificial intelligence, 18, 33, 54, 84, 105, 118, 140
astronomer, 42
attitude, 90
Aumann, R., 3
Austin, J.L., 25, 143
automata theory, 130
Avigad, J., 54
Awodey, S., 54
axiom
   of choice, 32, 35
   of determinacy, 35
   of infinity, 26
   of negative introspection, 22
   of positive introspection, 23
axiomatic analysis, 117

Index 155

axiomatic system, 21

backward induction, 4
bargaining, 1
Barwise, J., 109, 130
Basic Law V, 63
Bayart, A., 20
Bayesianism, 5, 49
behaviorism, 111
being, 137
belief, 21, 45, 46, 85, 91, 93, 103
   as proposition, 21
   as sentence-meaning, 21
   degree of, 49
   group, 17
   individual, 17
   report, 96
   revision, 55
Belnap, N., 94, 120
Bentham, J., 5
Bergson, H., 26
Berlin, 119
bilingualism, 105
Binmore, K., 1
biology, 26
bivalence, 138
Blackburn, P., 120
Blackburn, S., 103
Block, N., 99
Bloomfield, L., 111
Bolker, E., 53
Boltzmann, L., 110
Bonnay, D., 131
Boole, G., 61
Boston, 53
Brandom, R., 99
Brands, H., 119
Brooklyn, 13
Broome, J., 5
Brouwer, L.E.J., 35, 80, 95
Buffalo, 53
Bühler, A., 119

Bulgaria, 31
Burge, T., 145
Byrd, M., 13

calibration, 49
Cambridge University, 68
Camus, A., 137
Canberra, 42
Cantor, G., 79
Carmo, J., 24
Carnap, R., 14, 61, 110, 113, 144
Carnegie Mellon University, 51, 54
Carnielli, W., 10
Cartwright, R., 143
categorical grammar, 96
category, 95
category theory, 10, 11, 53, 57
Caton, C.E., 25
causal modeling, 44, 49
causation, 39, 43
chain-smoking, 129
chance, 42, 91
chemist, 42
Cherbourg, 2
Chisholm, R., 23
Chomsky, N., 105, 111, 130
Church, A., 79, 94, 124
Church's theorem, 62
circularity, 78
Coffa, A., 101
cognition, 77
cognitive ethology, 26
cognitive science, 47, 54, 92
Cohen, P., 2, 35
coherence, 126
Collingwood, R.G., 67
   An Autobiography, 67
Colyvan, M., 38
combinatorics, 98
commitment, 43

common-sense, 26, 43
communication, 19, 133
companion, 95
"comparative ignorance", 55
completeness, 123, 143
compositionality, 132
comprehension principle, 63
computation, 130, 133
computer, 105
computer program, 84
computer science, 33, 47, 84, 118
computer simulation, 47
concept, 32
conceptual analysis, 48, 117
"conceptual reconstruction", 144
conceptualization, 77
conditional, 39, 94
 counterfactual, 39, 94
 indicative, 90
 subjunctive, 3
conditional intent, 77
confirmation, 146
confirmation theory, 45, 49, 50
connective, 60
consciousness, 48
consequentialism, 68
consistency, 87, 126
constant, 28
 logical, 28, 131
 non-logical, 28, 131
constructivism, 137
constructivity, 126
content, 48
context, 27
 dialectical, 100
 negative, 131
 positive, 131
contextualism, 87
contingency, 10

continuity, 101
 Bolzano-Weierstrass, 101
continuum hypothesis, 2, 35, 62
conversation, 95
corroboration, 18
Costa-Leite, A., 9
countable additivity, 49
Cracow, 136
creativity, 38
credence, 49
curiosity, 147
cut-elimination, 123
Czeżowski, T., 135

Dąmbska, L., 136
database, 20
Datalog, 20
Davidson, D., 106
Davis, M., 117
 The Undecidable, 117
de Finetti, B., 14
de Rijke, M., 120
death, 11
Debreu, G., 1
 Theory of Value, 1
decidability, 84
decision problem, 40
decision theory, 5, 39, 40, 44, 48, 50, 51, 54
 behavioral, 55
 causal, 6, 51
 evidential, 51
Decock, L., 26
deduction, 27, 84, 106
defensibility, 87
definite description, 65, 93, 144
definition, 32, 78
 conservative, 100
Delsarte, Ph., 20
Demolombe, R., 20
deontology, 68
Department of Health, 146

Derrida, J., 140
desire, 45, 91
desire-as-belief thesis, 41
detachment, 147
determinism, 91, 137
diachronicity, 23
diagnosis, 18
diagonalization, 61, 62, 77
   semantic, 61
   set-theoretical, 61
   syntactical, 61
dialethism, 90
Diderot, D., 46
discourse
   rational, 60
   representation structure, 109
   representation theory, 96
discovery, 77
Dray, W., 142
Dreyfus, H., 148
Dummett, M., 95, 99

Earth-Moon system, 13
economics, 1, 25, 27, 54
   mathematical, 1
   micro-, 2
Edinburgh University, 117
education, 148
Eells, E., 13
egalitarianism, 4
Egan, A., 51
Einstein, A., 110
Ellsberg, D., 55
Elvis's Jungle Room, 39
Empire State Building, 39
empiricism, 48
empiricist, 79
encyclopedia, 95
Engel, P., 28
engineering, 47
English, 20
epistemic possibility, 85

epistemology, 3, 10, 21, 45, 54, 83, 85, 118, 124
   computational, 23
   probabilistic, 46
equilibrium, 4
ethics, 5, 17, 45, 48, 61, 133
   bio-, 140
   meta-, 51, 96, 103
   quasi-realism, 103
Euclid, 38
euthanasia, 79
existence, 137
existential, negative, 93
expectation, 55
expected utility, 40
experience, 26
experiment, 47
explanation, 143
   deductive-nomological, 143
   historical, 143
explanatory power, 126
expressability, 131
   non-, 131
   relative, 132
extension, 77
extensionalism, 68

Fackenheim, E., 141
Falkenberg, G., 119
fallacy, 145
fatalism, 138
Feferman, S., 131
fictionalist, 94
finite additivity, 49
Finnish-Soviet Logic Symposium, 119
Fisher, R.A., 44
Fitch, F., 125
Fitelson, B., 46
Fleck, L., 135
Fodor, J., 111
Føllesdal, D., 148
formal

linguistics, 118
formal epistemology, 14, 86, 91
formal methods, 11, 14, 32, 37, 54, 86, 93, 106, 119, 127, 130, 145
formal model, 55, 144, 146
formal philosophers, 148
formal reasoning, 3
formal system, 61
formalism, 38, 137
formalization, 20, 68, 71, 132
Forster, M., 13
Foundations of Measurement, 56
four colour problem, 20
Fox, C.R., 55
Free University of Berlin, 119
free will, 48, 148
Frege, G., 27, 35, 53, 60–62, 101, 112, 133
Grundgesetze der Arithmetik, 63
French, 20
friendship, 78
Frost, R., 113

Gabbay, D., 9, 119, 146
A Practical Logic of Cognitive Systems, 146
Agenda Relevance, 146
Fibring Logics, 9
The Reach of Abduction, 146
game, 51
 extensive form, 51
 normal form, 51
 of perfect information, 4
game theory, 2, 3, 5, 44, 49, 51
 evolutionary, 4
 foundations of, 3
 rational, 4

Gärdenfors, P., 119
Gaunillo, 46
generosity, 147
Gentzen, G.
 sequent calculus, 99
Gettier, E., 22, 87
Gettier problem, 22
Gillies, D., 17
 Philosophical Theories of Probability, 17
Ginzburg, L.A., 38
Gochet, P.
 Ascent to Truth, 28
 Outline of Nominalist Theory of Propositions, 27
God, 40, 48, 141, 148
Gödel, K., 35, 62, 79, 117, 118
 incompleteness theorems, 34, 48, 62, 117, 129, 130
Goldblatt, R., 10
good life, 78
Goodman, N., 16
Goranko, V., 31
grammar, 25
Grand Canyon, 39
graph, 105
 conceptual, 105, 109
 dependency, 105
 existential, 105
group theory, 120
guide, 95
Guillaume, A., 20

Hacking, I., 44
Hájek, A., 37
halting problem, 3, 79
handbook, 95
Hare, R., 5
Harmann, N., 25
Harper, B., 37

Harsanyi, J., 4, 5
Hart, H.L.A., 136
Harvard University, 112
Hegel, G., 117
Heidegger, M., 137, 140, 148
    Being and Time, 148
Helsinki, 119
Helzner, J., 53
Hempel, C.G., 14, 45, 143
Henderson, T.C., 19
Hendricks, V.F., 23, 48, 139
    Mainstream and Formal Epistemology, 23
    The Convergence of Scientific Knowledge, 23
Herstein, I.N., 56
Hilbert, D., 3, 35, 63
Hilbert's program, 61
Himalayas, 39
Hintikka, J., 20, 21, 86, 143
    Knowledge and Belief, 86, 143
Hume, D., 4, 9, 45
humility, 147
Husserl, E., 136, 148
hypothesis testing, 44

IBM, 105
idea, 112
idealism, 68
idealization, 14, 43, 91
identity, 45, 60
    propositional, 21
implication
    material, 90
    relevant, 90, 94
    strong, 21
indeterminism, 137
indexicality, 42, 108
induction, 26, 48
    mathematical, 26
inductivism, 45
inference, 95, 106

infinite regress, 77
infinity, 32, 77
information, 33, 107, 133
information theory, 47
informativity, 126
Ingarden, R., 136
inquiry, 111, 113
instrumentalist, 94
'intellectual intuition', 25
intension, 77
intensionalism, 68
intensionality, 109
intention, 27
intentionality, 77
intuition, 20, 98, 137
intuitionism, 95, 99
invalidity, 145

Jacquette, D., 59
Jagiellonian University, 135
Jago, M., 83
Jakobson, R., 111
James, W.
    Principles of Psychology, 111
Jeffrey, R., 14, 37, 53
Jones, A., 24
Jonsson, B., 19
just, 48
justification, 21, 86, 126
    'a first-class citizen', 21

Kadane, J.B., 39, 51
Kamp, H., 109
Kanger, S., 20, 148
    Collected Papers, 148
Kant, I., 4, 5, 35, 144, 148
Kantianism, 51
Kaplan, A., 21
Katz, J.J., 111
Keynes, J.M., 14
KK-thesis, 143
Kluwer, 148

Index

knowledge, 10, 33, 46, 72, 84, 85, 87, 91, 106, 113, 129, 133, 137
  as limiting convergence, 23
  as true justified belief, 21
  common, 3
Koch, R., 28
Kokoszyńska, M., 135
Kolmogorov, A.N., 39
Kotarbiński, T., 135
Krantz, D.H., 56
Kripke structure, 145
Kripke, S., 9, 11, 20, 109
Kyburg, H., 44

Ladrière, J., 29
Lakatos, I., 2
language, 19, 26, 64, 77, 95, 102, 106, 129, 133, 142
  formal, 132
  game, 19, 137
  learning, 105
  logical, 137
  mathematical, 63
  meta-, 35, 79, 112, 135
  natural, 9, 20, 93, 96, 102, 107, 123, 130, 132
  object, 35, 135
  programming, 105
  query, 20
  sensitivity, 16
  variance, 16
laptop, 47
Latour, B., 28, 94
law, 135, 148
Lawvere, F.W., 53
legal theory, 135
Leibniz, G.W.F., 6
Lemmon, E.J., 19
Lesniewskian mereology, 145
Levi, I., 51
Lewis, C.I., 113, 143
Lewis, D., 3, 37, 39
lexicography, 111, 114
life, purpose of, 12, 36
Lindström, P., 79, 129
linguistics, 25, 105, 111, 130
  computational, 105
  formal, 119
List, C., 51
literature, 148
Locke, J., 91
logic, 9, 14, 25, 31, 34, 53, 60, 64, 74, 77, 83, 93, 96, 98, 106, 114, 117, 118, 133
  aesthetics of, 77
  Aristotelian, 101
  categorical, 54
  classical, 49, 84, 100
  connexive, 125
  constructive, 84, 123, 126
  deontic, 23, 136
  epistemic, 10, 21, 72, 85, 118, 143
  extensional, 20, 64
  first-order, 19, 49, 62, 83, 89, 101, 102, 108, 125
  formal, 14, 32, 63, 114
  free, 144
  fuzzy, 84
  graphic, 107
  history of, 63
  inductive, 14, 15
  infinitary, 80
  informal, 145
  intensional, 20, 64
  intuitionistic, 84, 99, 123
  mathematical, 48, 53, 91
  meta-, 63
  modal, 14, 84, 94, 100, 102, 118, 120, 123, 143, 144

S5, 3, 100
S4, 143
T, 22
two-dimensional, 103
modal intuitionist, 145
modern, 60
moral parable, 61
non-classical, 120, 145
notation, 106
of fallacious reasoning, 145, 146
of plausibility, 146
paraconsistent, 84, 127
philosophical, 54, 61, 65, 98, 118, 137
primitive, 75
propositional, 19, 49
quantified connexive, 125
R, 94
relevant, 94
second-order, 83
substructural, 84, 127
syllogistic, 141
symbolic, 60, 65, 79
syntax, 59
temporal, 118
transfinitary, 80
truth-functional, 15
type-theoretical, 84
logic course, 13, 129
logical analysis, 117
logical atomism, 66, 142
logical empiricism, 140
logical equivalence, 20
logical form, 102, 142
logical monism, 126
logical omniscience, 21, 85
logical pluralism, 90
logical positivism, 110, 113
logician, 59, 94, 95, 145
philosophical, 118
logicism, 60, 137

"logocentrism", 145
London, 2
London School of Economics, 1
Chair of Mathematics, 1
Statistics Department, 1
Löwenheim, L., 79
Luce, R.D., 56
Lukasiewicz, J., 137, 138
Lvov-Warsaw School, 136

MacFarlane, J., 15
Mach, E., 110
Mackie, J., 5
Madison, 13
Maher, P., 16
Makinson, D., 119
Mares, E., 93
 Relevant Logic: A Philosophical Interpretation, 94
Martin-Löf, P., 99, 119
Marxism, 18
Massey, G., 47
mathematics, 1, 9, 13, 17, 31, 37, 53, 60, 93, 95, 97, 105, 144
aesthetics of, 77
applied, 78, 97
foundations of, 2, 32, 53, 105, 117, 118, 124, 137
meta-, 61
McCall, S., 125
meaning, 27, 48, 91, 99, 112, 123
measurement theory, 54
medicine, 18
memory, 84
mental fact, 45
Merleau-Ponty, M., 148
'metaphysical induction', 26
'metaphysical intuition', 26

metaphysician, 94
metaphysics, 10, 83, 102, 110
methodology, 45, 54, 95, 124
Mill, J.S., 5
Miller, D., 16
Milnor, J., 56
mind-body problem, 48, 79, 103
MIT, 105
"mixture space", 56
modal ideology, 102
modal operator, 122
modality, 10, 60, 103, 108
model
    conceptual, 146
    deductive, 16
    deterministic, 16
    non-deterministic, 16
    probabilistic, 16
model theory, 131
"models of data", 146
Mongin, Ph., 27
monotonicity, 131
Montague, R., 20, 105, 109
    'English as a Formal Language', 20
    Formal Philosophy, 20
moral
    absolutism, 5
    objectivity, 96
    psychology, 41
    standard, 96
Morgenstern, O., 2
Mostowski, A., 136
music, 53, 65
music composition, 53

Nagel, E., 117
Nanjing University, 18
Napoleon, 83
Nash equilibrium, 51
Nash, J., 4, 51
Nau, R., 51

necessity, 11
Neuhaus, F., 139
neurophysiology, 26
neuropsychology, 147
neuroscience, 92
Newman, J.R., 105, 117
    World of Mathematics, 105
Neyman, J., 44
Niiniluoto, I., 139
Nogina, E., 22, 86
non-entity, 93
non-triviality, 126
normalization, 49
Nover, H., 41
number
    cardinal, 80
    natural, 84
    ordinal, 80

object, 60
obligation, 24, 137
    actual, 24
    ideal, 24
ontic reduction, 77
ontological extravagance, 102
ontology, 11, 54, 114, 124
    formal, 60
Opałek, K., 136
oversimplification, 14
Oxford linguist analysis, 143
Oxford University, 67

$P =?NP$, 118
"paradigm-creep", 143
paradox, 65
    analysis, 127
    Chisholm, 23
    Curry, 65, 127
    Fitch, 9, 125
    Grelling, 65
    liar, 65
    logical, 65
    lottery, 46

Newcomb, 6
of knowability, 124
preface, 46
Pseudo-Scotus, 65
Russell, 65
self-referential, 34
St. Petersburg, 40
Zeno, 32
Parsons, T., 145
"partial belief", 55
Pasadena game, 41
Pasenkiewicz, K., 136
Peano, G., 61
Pearce, D., 119
Pearson, E., 44
Pedersen, S.A., 139
Peirce, C.S., 105, 111
 first rule of reason, 109
Perelman, C., 28
Perestroika, 119
permutation invariance, 28
Perry, J., 109
Peters, S.
 Quantifiers in Language and Logic, 130
Pettit, P., 42, 51
philosopher, 15, 42, 94, 101
philosophers, 14
philosophical pluralism, 140
philosophy, 1, 10, 14, 15, 19, 33, 53, 56, 60, 74, 83, 89, 93, 94, 96, 101, 105, 109, 117, 124, 130, 148
 academic, 4, 118
 Analytic, 25, 94, 112, 119, 140
 and descriptive questions, 43
 and prescriptive questions, 43
 anti-, 78
 as an island, 25
 as Calculus Ratiocinator, 34
 as pre-science, 4
 as promontory, 25
 as reflection, 132
 'by frission', 20
 Continental, 25, 140, 141, 148
 formal, 54, 93
 heuristics, 42
 history of, 142
 mainstream, 87
 meta-, 47
 moral, 4, 23
 of _ _, 43
 of astronomy, 43
 of biology, 4, 43, 124
 of category theory, 95
 of chemistry, 124
 of geology, 43
 of history, 95
 of information theory, 47
 of language, 95, 132
 of logic, 80, 89
 of mathematics, 4, 11, 17, 18, 26, 35, 57, 95, 124, 140
 of meteorology, 43
 of mind, 25, 45, 103, 140
 of physics, 13, 43
 of science, 13, 16–18, 95, 136
 of statistics, 44
 ordinary language, 137, 143
 political, 4
 scientific, 109
 theoretical, 60
 without tears, 143
philosophy department, 15
photographer, 59

photography, 59
physicist, 42
physics, 13, 18, 48, 93, 111
   history of, 13
   mathematical, 13, 14
picture theory, 66
Pittsburgh, 54
Plato, 2, 5, 21, 35, 48, 62
   Republic, 2
   Theaetetus, 21
Platonism, 35, 95
poetry, 114
Poker, 2
polarity item, 131
politics, 65
Popper, K., 2, 9, 14, 18, 45
   The Open Society and its Enemies, 2
positivism, 143
Post-Modernism, 28
post-modernist, 94
potentiality, 77
pragmatics, 95
Prawitz, D., 99
predication, 60
predictive accuracy, 16
preference, 49
Priest, G., 90, 98
Princeton University, 37, 53
principle
   of indifference, 50
   of maximum entropy, 50
   Principal, 50
   Reflection, 50
Prior, A., 14
Prisoners' Dilemma, 6
probability, 14, 45
   conditional, 39, 49
   foundations of, 14
   interpretation of, 18
   intersubjective, 17
   subjective, 50

probability theory, 37, 39, 49, 98
   logical, 50
   subjective, 50
problem-solving capacity, 126
proof, 118, 130, 146
   axiom-theorem format, 3
proof theory, 99, 120
proof-net, 99
property, 42, 60
proposition, 21, 103, 108
Proust, J., 26
Przegląd Filozoficzny, 135
psyche, 111
psychology, 25, 111
   cognitive, 111
   experimental, 26
   moral, 45
"pure wool", 148

qualia, 77
quantification, 101, 106
quantifier, 60
quantum mechanics, 13, 91, 137
Quine, W.V., 61, 89, 102, 144
   Set Theory and Its Logic, 26
   Theories and Things, 28
   'Two Dogmas of Empiricism', 26
   Word and Object, 19

Ramses II, 28
Ramsey, F.P., 55, 64
   "Truth and Probability", 55
ratio analysis, 39
rational
   bargaining, 4
   choice, 55
   decision, 4
   decision-making, 41

judgement, 49
player, 3
preference, 3
super-, 117
rationalism, 48
rationality, 3, 48, 49, 51, 54, 90
Rautenberg, W., 119
Rawls, J., 4
difference principle, 4
realism, 68, 120, 123
reality, 25, 93
reasoning, 34, 64, 83, 93, 101, 106, 133, 146
reducibility, 45
reference, 93
Regularity, 50
relation, 108
relativism, 15, 28
religion, 60, 65
replacement theorem, 125
Restall, G., 90, 97
restricted complement thesis, 122
revisionist, 95
Reyle, U., 109
Roget, P.M., 111
Rott, H., 55
Royaumont, 25
Russell, B., 17, 24, 27, 35, 53, 60–62, 65, 93, 110, 112, 117, 142
Introduction to Mathematical Philosophy, 117
Principia Mathematica, 117

Sarkar, S., 46
Saussure, F.d., 111
Savage, L., 4
Scheffler, U., 139
Schervish, M.J., 39, 51
Schopenhauer, A., 77

science, 4, 9, 17, 19, 26, 60, 65, 91, 94
foundations of, 16
natural, 64
scientific method, 26
'scientism', 94
scope
distinction, 93
security, 55
Seidenfeld, T., 39, 51, 54
semantic network, 105
semantics, 14, 35, 64, 94, 96, 99, 103, 105, 111, 130, 135, 136
algebraic, 19
compositional, 93
event, 106
formal, 14, 19
"Gentzen", 123
Kripke, 14
Meinongean, 144
modal, 103
neighborhood, 54
possible world, 3, 11, 12, 20, 85, 94, 102
proof-theoretic, 123
relational, 54
situation, 109
supervaluational, 144
semiotics, 111
set, 11, 95
convex, 54
non-well-founded, 94
set theory, 11, 24, 35, 38, 60, 98, 145
Zermelo-Fraenkel, 32, 62
Shakespeare, W., 59
Simon, H., 54
simplicity, 126
Sinclair, A., 141
Sintonen, M., 139
skepticism, 46

Skolem, T., 79
Skyrms, B., 6, 14, 51
Sleeping Beauty, 49
Smith, B.E., 114
Sober, E., 13
Socratic wisdom, 22
software system, 105
soul, immortality of, 148
soundness, 46, 143
Sowa, J.F., 105
space, 48
speech-act, 103
Spinoza, B.d., 38
Springer, 148
St. Anselm, 46
St. Augutine
 Confessions, 141
Stalnaker, R., 39, 41
statistical mechanics, 110
statistician, 1
statistics, 37, 44, 49
 Bayesian, 44
 classical, 44
 foundations of, 54
stit theory, 122
strategic interaction, 51
Strawson, P.F., 107
strict finitism, 95
strong negation, 123
structure, 142
Studia Logica, 136
Sukale, M., 119
supervenience, 45
Suppes, P., 56, 146
Suppes-Noll theory, 145
Surma, S., 136
syllogism, 142
syllogistic, 125
Symons, J., 48
synchronicity, 23
synonymy, 21, 27
syntax, 99, 105, 130, 135

Syracuse, 13

Tampere, 119
Tan, Y.-H., 120
Tarski, A., 19, 35, 61, 79, 135, 139
Technical University Wrocław, 136
Tennant, N., 99, 125
Tesnière, L., 105
Thayse, A., 20
theism, 40
theorem, 146
 deduction, 90
 prover, 20
 proving, 105
 representation, 49
theoretical physicist, 13
theory formation, 120
thermo-dynamics, 120
Thijsse, E., 120
Thomason, R., 20
thought experiment, 55
time, 32, 48, 108, 133
topology, 53, 98, 146
topos theory, 54
torture, 3
tractability, 126
truth, 28, 48, 60, 91, 126, 130, 139
 analytic, 26
 context-bond, 28
 synthetic, 19, 26
tuberculosis, 28
Turing, A., 3, 79, 117, 130
Tversky, A., 55, 56
Twardowski, K., 136
type label, 107
type theory, 24

uncertainty principle, 137
undecidability, 83
understanding, 98

Index   167

University of Düsseldorf, 119
University of Göteborg, 129
University of Michigan, 143
University of Queensland, 97
University of Toronto, 141
University of Western Ontario, 37
University of Wisconsin, 13
Ur-Logik, 75
utilitarianism, 4, 5

validity, 84, 145
van Benthem, J., 21, 28, 120, 130, 131
van der Hoek, W., 120
van der Meyden, R., 22
van Fraassen, B., 37
Vanderveken, D., 21
Venema, Y., 120
verisimilitude, 16
voluntarism, 120
   doxastic, 120
von Kutschera, F., 123
von Neumann, J., 2, 118
   Theory of Game and Economic Behavior, 2
von Wright, G.H., 119
Vuillemin, J., 24

Wager, P., 39
Wahl, J., 25
Walton, D., 145
Wang, H., 113
   Beyond Analytic Philosophy, 113
Wansing, H., 119, 139
Westerståhl, D., 129
   Quantifiers in Language and Logic, 130
Whitehead, A.N., 26, 109, 110, 141
Willaschek, M., 120
William James Lecture, 112

William of Ockham, 26
Williams, B., 24
Williamson, T., 125
Wilson, J.C., 67
Wittgenstein, L., 61, 62, 66, 78, 93, 130, 139
   Notebooks 1914–1916, 66
   Philosophical Investigations, 19
   Tractatus, 9, 19, 66, 112
Wójcicki, R., 120
Wolenski, J., 135
Wolter, W., 135
Woods, J., 141
   The Logic of Fiction, 144
Woods-Walton approach, 145
Woolf, R., 53
World 3, 18
world-views, 127
Wundt, W., 111

Zheng, Y., 18

www.ingramcontent.com/pod-product-compliance
Lightning Source LLC
Chambersburg PA
CBHW031630160426
43196CB00006B/353